Containing Beauty
Japanese Bamboo Flower Baskets

Containing Beauty
Japanese Bamboo Flower Baskets

Text by Toshiko M. McCallum
Design by Jung-yu S. Lien

UCLA Museum of Cultural History

This volume is dedicated to the memory of Arnold Rubin.

Front Cover. Flower basket (*hanakago*) with handle. 38.5 cm. Lent by Helen and Robert Kuhn. See also Plate 27.

Museum of Cultural History
University of California, Los Angeles
405 Hilgard Avenue
Los Angeles, California 90024

This volume was made possible by funding from the Ahmanson Foundation, the Neutrogena Corporation, Helen and Robert Kuhn, the National Endowment for the Humanities, and Manus, the support group of the Museum of Cultural History.

ISBN 0-930741-15-3 (hardcover)
ISBN 0-930741-16-1 (softcover)
Library of Congress Catalog Card No. 88-50730

Published in conjunction with an exhibition at UCLA Museum of Cultural History, Haines Hall Gallery 2.

Sunday, July 17 - Sunday, September 18, 1988.

Table of Contents

Foreword

It has been a longstanding priority of the Museum of Cultural History to integrate exhibition and publication projects with the academic interests of UCLA graduate students. This project is unique in that it combines the diverse interests of two students, Toshiko M. McCallum from the Department of Anthropology and Jung-yu S. Lien from the Design area of the Department of Art, Design and Art History. Toshiko McCallum interrupted her studies to conduct the necessary research both here and in Japan and to author this volume. Her interviews with contemporary Japanese basket makers have added a major dimension to the scope of this project. Jung-yu Lien supervised the photography, developed all the graphics, and designed both the exhibition and this volume as part of her Master of Fine Arts degree. Her sensitive handling of the aesthetic dimensions of *Containing Beauty* have made an appealing subject even more approachable. It has been a rare pleasure to work with a scholar and an artist who share a commitment to excellence.

The impetus for *Containing Beauty* came from several people. The late Dr. Arnold Rubin, to whom this volume is dedicated, lit the initial spark and offered key ideas at early stages. A spectacular gift of eighty baskets from Nancy and Richard Bloch made the potential exhibition a reality. It was Professor Jack Carter's inspiration to have one of his graduate students undertake the display and publication design as an M.F.A. project. Substantial loans from Helen and Robert Kuhn and Lloyd E. Cotsen, Chief Executive Officer of the Neutrogena Corporation, increased the breadth of styles and techniques represented here. In addition Helen added her keen eye to the selection process along with many helpful suggestions. Karyn Zarubica of Neutrogena patiently handled our many requests with efficiency and enthusiasm. Belinda Sweet, on short notice, also agreed to lend to the exhibition. The Museum thanks all of the above for the time and interest they have given. As always the Museum staff provided the vital support necessary for the success of this project. Henrietta Cosentino extended her role as editor and coordinated several aspects of the production.

Funding for this volume was generously provided by the Ahmanson Foundation, the National Endowment for the Humanities, Helen and Robert Kuhn, and Manus, the support group of the Museum of Cultural History. Institutional support for this and indeed all Museum undertakings can be traced directly to Vice Chancellor Elwin V. Svenson and Chancellor Charles E. Young.

Christopher B. Donnan, Director
Doran H. Ross, Associate Director

Acknowledgments

Many splendid Japanese bamboo flower baskets can be found in the collections of museums, art lovers, and patrons of the tea ceremony. Yet strangely, given their popularity, they have been studied very little. The 1985 exhibition at the National Museum of Modern Art, Tokyo, and its catalogue represented the first effort since World War II to focus on them in a comprehensive way. As we planned for the Museum of Cultural History publication and its accompanying exhibition, we found little information in the United States on the subject. Thus it was decided to interview basket makers living in Japan. Though research was limited to three weeks, the short trip yielded a great deal of valuable information, thanks to a number of distinguished Japanese artists whom Toshiko M. McCallum had the privilege of interviewing in September, 1987.

Iizuka Shōkansai, who holds the honored status of Living National Treasure, took time out from his exceptionally busy schedule for a lengthy interview. His patient and insightful explanations were fundamental in helping formulate ideas on this subject. Ikeda Hyōa, a specialist in the making of baskets associated with the tea ceremony, provided invaluable information and kindly shared his research on the history of tea ceremony basketry. His sons Ikeda Iwao, a lacquer artist, and Ikeda Kiyoshi, a young bamboo artist, were helpful, too. Gratitude is owed to several people in the Kyoto-Osaka area. Hayakawa Shōkosai, descended from a long line of master basket makers, demonstrated traditional methods of bamboo preparation that have been handed down strictly from father to son in his family. Two generations of the Tanabe family were most cordial in their assistance: Tanabe Shōchiku, who is both a serious student of Kansai basketry and an innovative artist in his own right, gave a lengthy interview and provided important documentary material. He also arranged meetings with his father Tanabe Chikuunsai II, who has strongly influenced the development of bamboo arts in the Kansai region, and with his brother Tanabe Yōta, a leader of the avant-garde in basketry. All the artists were particularly generous in sparing precious time during their busiest month, when they prepare for the important fall exhibitions. Their wives, too, extended warm hospitality. Conversations with these distinguished men were a primary source for this volume. All direct quotations are taken from those interviews, and translated by Toshiko M. McCallum. Their names appear in the normal Japanese order, with family name first. Most bamboo artists take a professional name to use in place of their given one—a practice respected in this volume.

Helen and Robert Kuhn made their baskets available for study and Helen assisted in the selection for the exhibition. Lloyd E. Cotsen, President of the Neutrogena Corporation, gave us access to the Neutrogena collection and Karyn Zarubica, its curator, kindly assisted our study of the works under her supervision. We deeply appreciate the generosity of these lenders.

Many others assisted in this project. Eiichi Hamanishi, Director of the Los Angeles office of the Japan Foundation, was as always most cooperative. Shiraishi Kazumi, of the Traditional Craft section of the Agency for Cultural Affairs, was very helpful from the start and provided crucial research material in Tokyo. Moroyama Masanori, of the Craft section of the Tokyo National Museum of Modern Art, shared useful information on all aspects of bamboo arts. Sagami Akira, owner of Chikuhan Shōten, a store specializing in bamboo, offered a practical perspective on the nature of the material for craft purposes. Inoue Yōichi, Assistant Curator in the Archaeology Department (Prehistoric Age Section), Tokyo National Museum, kindly supplied photographs of Jōmon pottery. Kuroiwa Kyōsuke, at the Kita Kyushu Municipal Museum of Art, gave information about Kyushu baskets. Sōsei Matsumoto, Los Angeles tea master, allowed us to photograph her tea room alcove and arranged flowers for its adornment. Robert Hori, Gallery Director for the Japanese American Cultural Center, assisted in its decoration and explained tea utensils. Ryōko Shibata did the calligraphy for the cover. A number of friends helped with sundry questions and problems, including Yasuo Sakata, Mariko LaFleur, Mihoko Miki, Vicki Botz, Yoko Collier-Sanuki, Lynn Anderson, Rachel Hoffman, and James C. Cuno. We are indebted to Michael Cohen for custom-designing a macron.

The Museum of Cultural History deserves very special thanks for its tireless assistance in this project. In the past year, under the supervision of Christopher Donnan and Doran H. Ross, many have given generous time and energy to the project. Registrar Sarah Jane Kennington and Catharine Swan, Assistant Registrar, sorted, accessioned, and kept track of a seemingly endless number of baskets, and Collections Manager Robert V. Childs and his Assistant Owen Moore helped manage the assemblage. Richard Todd spent untold days in the dark room doing the beautiful studio photography, and also offered helpful advice on documentary photography in Japan. Senior Exhibition Preparator Don Simmons and Assistant Exhibition Designer Carl Eugene Riggs worked hard to mount the exhibit accompanying this volume. Betsy Quick ably coordinated publicity, developed educational programs, and kindly gave over much of her workspace to the preparations for this volume. She and Patricia Altman were a valued source of technical craft expertise, and Phillip M. Douglas made important library books available. Sarah Kennington and Verni Greenfield read the manuscript and provided useful comments. Millicent Besser masterminded financial matters. Richard Chute's daily computer assistance was invaluable. Henrietta Cosentino's careful editing helped transform the manuscript into readable English and her patient queries and suggestions contributed greatly to the development of this book. Behind the scenes, Barbara Underwood and Betsy Escandor helped us constantly. To Professor Jack Carter, whose design expertise and moral support were crucial, our gratitude is immense. We are likewise deeply indebted to Doran H. Ross, Associate Director, who has advised, encouraged, and guided us from start to finish.

The cooperation of the Departments of Anthropology and of Art, Design, and Art History has been crucial to the success of this endeavor, and several department members deserve to be recognized. Dr. Clement W. Meighan, Toshiko McCallum's advisor, has given constant support, as have Dr. James R. Sackett and Dr. Wendell H. Oswalt of the Department of Anthropology. High praise and gratitude likewise go to Jung-yu Lien's M.F.A. committee, chaired by Professor William C. Brown and including Professors Kathleen Bick, Jack Carter, Mitsuru Kataoka, and Doran H. Ross. We are also very thankful to Dr. Donald F. McCallum, art historian, for his critical contributions to the manuscript. Special tribute should be paid to the late Dr. Arnold Rubin for his initial inspiration. Arnold, with his customary sensitivity and curiosity, realized the potential for a display of Japanese bamboo flower baskets. From the beginning he was a constant source of advice and stimulation.

Closer to home, we would like to thank our families, and especially our husbands, for their unending patience, counsel, help, and good cheer. This volume and its accompanying exhibition depended on the fine efforts of many. Their contributions constitute an important step toward understanding an art form that has not yet received the attention it deserves.

Toshiko M. McCallum
Jung-yu S. Lien

Prologue

"Once upon a time there lived an old bamboo cutter. Every day he would make his way into the fields and mountains to gather bamboo, which he fashioned into all manner of things. This old man was called Sanuki no Miyakko. One day he noticed a light at the root of a bamboo stalk and, thinking that this was very strange, went over to examine it. He saw that the light shone inside the hollow bamboo, where a most fetching little girl about three inches tall was sitting...." (Keene 1956:330).

So begins The Tale of the Bamboo Cutter (Taketori monogatari), *written in the late ninth or early tenth century and considered to be the oldest story in Japanese literature. The child is so tiny that the old man and his wife raise her in a bamboo basket. When fully grown and radiant with beauty, she is given the name Nayotake no Kaguyahime, "Shining Princess of Young Bamboo." But she belongs to the Moon People, and in the end must return to her home.*

This story eloquently expresses the Japanese sentiment toward bamboo. Clean, noble, and mysterious, it is perfectly suited to cradle the heavenly Moon Princess who descends for a time to earth.

13

Basketry
and the Art of
Flower Arrangement

The Japanese people have always shown a keen sensitivity to the change of seasons. To bring the seasonal mood into the household they display flowers associated with the various times of year, and often choose to place them in containers fashioned of bamboo. Free, naturalistic compositions seem especially appropriate to bamboo baskets, which have a softer and more relaxed quality than vases made of glass, porcelain, or bronze.

Beyond the realm of flower display, bamboo is used in a multitude of ways, and has long played a crucial role in the life of the Japanese people. In traditional mudwalled houses it provided the wattling as well as the furniture within. Musical instruments, especially flutes of all sizes, are made of bamboo. It has been the customary material for tools and utensils as diverse as laundry poles and fish traps, tea whisks and rakes (Pl. 1). Bamboo ladders, valued for their strength and light weight, are still very much in use; electricians, for example, mount them to repair the wires of Japan's famous bullet trains—a remarkable conjunction of ancient and advanced technologies (Ueda 1979:21).

Bamboo baskets, used for containment, storage, decoration, and display, have a particularly long history of development. A basket dating from the late Jōmon period was found in the Shinpukuji shell midden in Saitama Prefecture (Ogasawara 1985:299). It was shallow and mat plaited, with very narrow bamboo strips, and bore a thick layer of lacquer on its surface. Baskets of this type, sealed with lacquer so as to

be water tight, are called *rantai-shikki*. Many have been excavated from sites of the late Jōmon period, as have a number of unlacquered baskets. The literature is vague about what material they are made from, except in the case of the Shinpukuji basket, which is clearly described as bamboo. Most *rantai-shikki* were twill plaited. The impress of basketry on the surfaces of Jōmon pottery has revealed many kinds of plaiting, suggesting a high level of technical development in this early period (Fig. 1). Twill and mat plaiting are very ancient techniques.

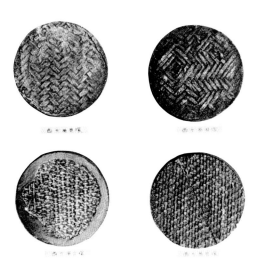

Figure 1. Plaitings appear on pots from Nishigahara shell midden, Tokyo, ca. 2,000-1,000 B.C. (Late Jōmon period). Facsimiles courtesy of the Archaeological Museum, Kokugakuin University, Tokyo.

Plate 1.

More than five hundred bamboo baskets from the Nara period (A.D. 710-794) are still housed at the Shōsōin, the ancient imperial treasure house where an eighth-century art and craft collection is preserved (Mizuo 1970:80). The treasure house stands on the grounds of Tōdaiji, the imperial temple in Nara, the capital city of that period. The Shōsōin baskets are plain and shallow; they have no handles. Apparently the majority were used to hold flower petals which were scattered during religious ceremonies at the Tōdaiji.

It is not yet clear when bamboo baskets were first used to display flowers, but it seems likely that this function had its roots in the tea ceremony and the art of flower arrangement, both of which developed during the Muromachi period (A.D. 1333-1573). The use of flowers as an aspect of interior decoration achieved a mature formulation in the fifteenth century (Yamane 1987:15-23). Great numbers of Chinese items such as paintings, vases, and glazed ceramics, especially *tenmoku* and celadon, were imported during this time. Called *karamono* ("Chinese objects"), they were highly valued by the Ashikaga shoguns and the aristocracy in the capital city, Kyoto. The elite mansions of that period were built in the architectural style called *shoin-zukuri* (lit., "study style" but often translated as "reception-room style"), so named

16 because they featured a study-like room (*shoin*) devoted to culture. Here they held parties to display their *karamono* ware, and the exotic Chinese vases of bronze, brass, glass, and celadon bestowed on their owners the greatest prestige.

At first the vases were exhibited by themselves, but gradually flowers were added to enhance their beauty. Specialists appeared and refined the new art, called *rikka* (lit., "to stand flowers," based on a reading of characters borrowed from the Chinese), and they developed guidelines for the creation of complicated floral arrangements (Pls. 2,3). At some point baskets as well as vases began to be used for these displays. A seventeenth-century tea ceremony document of the early Edo period (A.D. 1615-1868) claims that Shogun Ashikaga Yoshimasa (1436-90) was the first to use a basket specifically for flowers (Ikeda 1980:195). But since the report postdates the shogun by nearly two centuries, the truth of the matter remains uncertain. The container depicted in Plate 2 was probably made of metal; but its shape—that of a "hanging boat" (*tsuribune*)—may have inspired basket makers, for many later baskets have been and are still fashioned in *tsuribune* form.

The term *ikebana* (from *ike*, "to arrange, to give new life," and from *hana*, "flowers") did not come into use until the Edo period, when the

湖龍圖

Plate 4.

merchant class achieved great economic power and attempted to emulate the lifestyle of the traditional elite by adopting aristocratic art forms (Ōi 1964:108-118). A woodcut from this period shows a courtesan and her attendant arranging chrysanthemums in a basket vase for the autumn festival of Chōyō (Pl. 4). Since in cities like Edo and Osaka many more people belonged to the merchant class than to the ruling samurai class, their enthusiastic patronage of flower arrangement prompted the development of various "schools," each devoted to a distinct philosophy, and each with its own rules of arrangement. In response to the popularity of the art among a wider segment of the population, simpler and less artificial forms of display were devised and the term *ikebana* appeared in popular parlance. With the emergence of modern Japan in the Meiji period (A.D. 1868-1912), interest in the art expanded to a much broader population.

The *Tokonoma*

Traditionally flower arrangements are put in the alcove, or *tokonoma*, the most formal place in a Japanese house. The alcove appeared during the Muromachi period as an architectural feature of the *shoin*. It was a secular development of what had originally been a religious corner in the home, typically consisting of an altar with candle, incense, and flower offerings, placed before a Buddhist scroll. This format provided the basis for the aesthetic adornment of a special space

17

18

Plate 5. *Left.*
Plate 6. *Right.*

constructed within the *shoin*. A woodcut by the master print maker, Harunobu, shows a *tokonoma* from the Edo period, with clearly secular decorations and *ikebana* (Pl. 5).

The contemporary *tokonoma* is a raised alcove situated in one corner of the drawing room (*zashiki*), where guests are entertained and important family ceremonies such as weddings and special birthdays are celebrated (Pl. 6). A scroll (*kakejiku*) with a painting or calligraphy is hung on the wall and changed as appropriate according to the season or the specific occasion for which the room is to be used. *Ikebana*, usually in combination with an incense burner, an ornamental sculpture, or both, is placed in the alcove.

It is very important that the hanging scroll and other objects in the *tokonoma* be in harmony. When a very formal scroll is used for a special occasion, the other elements, including the flower arrangement and its container, should manifest the same degree of formality. In other words, the *tokonoma* expresses the artistic sensibility of the household. During our conversation, Iizuka Shōkansai related his reaction on visiting a certain house:

> ... when I visited this house, I was very sur-
> prised at the arrangement of the tokonoma.
> On the hanging scroll was calligraphy from a
> Buddhist sutra. There was an incense burner
> with a handle of the type used by monks in
> Buddhist ceremonies. The flower vase was an

Ikebana and Basketry Today

Today *ikebana* is one of the accomplishments most prized in young women of marriageable age. High schools and colleges have flower arrangement clubs as an extra-curricular activity. Big companies with large numbers of female employees provide free *ikebana* lessons. Business offices, restaurants, the waiting rooms of hospitals, and other public places are adorned with flowers. The students and followers of the many "schools" hold annual shows to exhibit examples of their work.

Prior to World War II, bamboo baskets were favored for *ikebana*. Nowadays they are clearly less popular than ceramic and glass vases, which are very common merchandise in department stores. According to Ikeda Hyōa, one reason for this is that more abstract flower arrangements, incorporating inorganic objects and dried plants, became quite popular after the war; and for this genre, a ceramic vase of modern design is more appropriate than a basket. Nevertheless it seems that baskets are beginning to regain their position. Though many forms of bamboo craft may disappear, Hyōa predicts that flower baskets and other items made for interior decoration will continue to be produced in the modern world.

There are three broad categories of artistic bamboo objects used for flower arrangement. The first is made from a single, fine, polished bamboo tube, cut so as to incorporate the sealed floor of one segment, which holds the water and the flowers. Technically called *marutakemono*, literally "a thing [made] of bamboo tube," it must be distinguished from the unfinished tube-

19

exquisite Chinese white porcelain. Everything was of the utmost formality. So I asked the master of the house about the reason for this arrangement, and he was glad I recognized it, and explained that this day was one year after the death of a teacher whom he had highly respected. In memory of this teacher he had decorated the tokonoma *in this manner.*

Although the *tokonoma* is the place for carefully composed flower arrangements, more modest ones can be placed in the living room, entrance hall, and even the bathroom. Nowadays since many Japanese houses have been westernized, and because they are generally less spacious than previously, the *tokonoma* is frequently omitted. Nevertheless the art of flower arrangement is still important.

Plate 7.

containers used inside baskets, which go by a different name and are not considered objects of fine art. The *marutakemono* is often used for flowers in the tea ceremony; then, however, it is called *hanaire*, a general description meaning "flower container," but also the term used for any class of the tea ceremony flower holder. In the second category are containers made of rather narrow non-interactive bamboo tubes, and termed *marutake kumimono*, literally "a thing constructed from bamboo tubes" (Pl. 7). Since this kind is not watertight, a water and flower holder must be placed inside.

Henso, the third category, is the technical term for objects made by the interworking of elements. Baskets are more popularly known as *hanakago*, literally, "flower basket." This category allows great variety, depending on the width and thickness of bamboo strips, the modulation of form, the arrangement and combination of plaiting and twining techniques, and the dyeing of the basket as a whole or in parts. It comprises the majority of baskets considered here. Within the category of *henso* or *hanakago* there is no standard classification system. A basket may be referred to in terms of its special features (such as the presence of a handle), its distinctive shape (should it look, for example, like a gourd, a boat, or a fishing basket), or its particular method of construction. Moreover since it has been traditional to copy famous baskets—especially those imported from China—the original basket name is frequently borrowed as well.

Basket makers sometimes have their own ways of categorizing their work. Iizuka Shōkansai's father, Rōkansai (1890-1958), who played a very important role in the modernization of bamboo art, classified baskets in terms of their formality according to three categories: *shin*, *gyō*, and *sō*. As Shōkansai explained:

The most formal type basket, shin, has a symmetrical form with precise, elaborate 'weaves'. It takes a long time to make, and the basket itself is a fine art object even without an arrangement of flowers. Gyō is the middle range. The basket work is more relaxed than for shin baskets, although the form is still symmetrical. The sō type utilizes rough 'weaves', and various interesting modulations of shape can be seen in this category.

This classification system, a traditional one originating with calligraphy, has also been applied to painting, flower arrangement, the architectural styles of the *tokonoma*, and the daily activities of the Japanese people. Shōkansai feels it provides a clear framework when he plans a new basket; it also helps establish the appropriate flower arrangement. For a *shin* basket, plants of high status, such as pine, peony, and chrysanthemum, are arranged in a very formal manner. The *gyō* type is very adaptable because it allows both formal and relaxed ways of displaying flowers, although there is a certain degree of restriction. A *sō* basket is best for a spontaneous, free-style arrangement.

Figure 2. The lid of a tea ceremony
utensil box shows the name of the basket
made by Ikeda Hyōa.

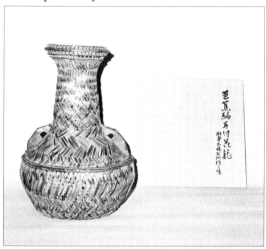

Basketry
and the
Tea Ceremony

The development of flower basketry in Japan is closely related to the history of the tea ceremony. Ritual tea-drinking had its origins in the Buddhist monasteries of China and Japan. During the later Muromachi period it was taken up by the shoguns and the aristocracy, and ultimately by the broader population. In its original and most lasting form, the ceremony revolved, as it does today, around the preparation and drinking of a powdered green tea (*matcha*). Hot water was added directly to tea powder in the drinking bowl, and mixed with a tea whisk; thus the ceremony was known as *chanoyu* (lit., "tea in hot water"). It was also called chadō (lit., "way of tea") since each step of the ritual was governed by strict rules of etiquette and encoded a philosophy of life. A different ceremony known as *senchadō* (lit., "way of *sencha*"), using brewed green-leaf tea (*sencha*) instead of powder, evolved about two centuries later and enjoyed great popularity up until the Second World War, when it fell somewhat out of fashion. Today, therefore, when people speak of the tea ceremony, it is likely to be *chanoyu*.

The later Muromachi period, when *chanoyu* took shape, was one of great importance for the political and cultural history of Japan. The role of *chanoyu* can hardly be exaggerated, for it contributed to the establishment of various cultural forms commonly thought of as distinctly Japanese. Indeed many historians feel that the entire complex of objects and behavior associated with *chanoyu* represent a fundamen-

tal expression of Japanese aesthetic taste. Beyond that, it is the source of much historical documentation, since the masters and patrons of the ceremony customarily kept written records of each event they hosted, including details such as guests' names, time of day, food served, and arrangement of hanging scroll, flowers, and utensils. Ikeda Hyōa pointed out that the tea ceremony milieu also contributed to the physical preservation of Japanese culture. Important utensils of the tea ceremony have been carefully wrapped in cotton cloth and then stored in wooden boxes. Made from organic material, the flower baskets and tea ceremony utensils would have been destroyed long ago if people had not preserved them with such loving care. Furthermore, written on the lid of the box there are important data about the contents within, for example the names of the object, maker (if known), and owner(s) of the piece (Fig. 2). Some of this information, several hundred years old, is extremely important historical documentation.

Chanoyu developed under the patronage of the Kyoto aristocracy, the same group associated with the beginnings of flower arrangement. Indeed *chanoyu* and flower arrangement can be said to have had a parallel development, although their exact connection is not well documented. As earlier noted, these aristocrats had parties in their *shoin* to show off their Chinese imports. It was there, too, that they held the *chanoyu*, and thus often referred to it as *shoin-cha*, or "study-room tea." The objects they used in the tea ceremony were predominantly Chinese (Fujioka

21

Plate 8 a,b.

22   1968:17-18). These would have included tea
cups and tea-powder containers, for example, as
well as the flower vases already discussed.

We do not know how early or to what extent
baskets were among the imported goods. Even
though some *karamono* baskets are said to date
from the Muromachi period, there is no definite
evidence of this. Historical investigation of
karamono baskets has not been sufficient, and it
is hoped that future research will reveal more

about their impact on the Japanese flower basket
tradition. While the Edo period document
discussed earlier claims that Shogun Ashikaga
Yoshimasa used a basket for flower arrangements, it does not state the context. Yet it is
highly probable that *karamono* baskets were
imported and used in a *chanoyu* context, along
with other imports, since they have been traditionally considered to belong to the category of
utensils for the *shoin-cha*.

In any case, throughout the centuries patrons
collected splendid *karamono* baskets. At the
same time numerous fine replicas of the Chinese
style were produced by master Japanese basket
makers, and these, too, were highly prized and
collected. *Karamono* baskets are made with
precise, elaborate interworkings of thin and
narrow bamboo strips. In form they are usually
symmetrical and often have handles. Fine
decoration of wrapping and knots is characteris-

tically applied with rattan around the rim and handle (Ikeda 1980:194-195). The baskets shown in Plate 8 are typical of Japanese-made *karamono* style; Plate 8b is an example of the famous form called Reishōjo. Tanabe Shōchiku explained that Reishōjo was a legendary young Chinese maiden, a paragon of filial duty. She supported her old parents by selling bamboo utensils made by her father, and achieved enlightenment through Zen Buddhism. Basket makers worshiped her as the founding goddess of their occupation, and up until about World War II, performed periodic rituals to honor her. There is not a single first-rate contemporary basket maker who has not copied *karamono* baskets. Mastery of its delicate techniques is an important part of the training process, and *karamono* methods have been integrated into the distinctively Japanese styles that developed later.

The Emergence of Domestic Style

As time passed, changes took place in *chanoyu*. While ceremonies continued to be held in the richly appointed mansions of the aristocracy, some tea masters began to seek the tranquil, spiritual beauty of a simple ceremony in humble surroundings. This transformation, begun by Murata Shukō and Takeno Jō-ō, was completed by the great tea master Sen no Rikyū, who lived from 1521 to 1591 (Fujioka 1968:18). Although he was also a master of the aristocratic *shoin-cha*, Rikyū chose to set his ceremony in a plain grass hut (*sōan*). For his "grass hut tea," or *sōan-cha*,

he adopted simple native artifacts as utensils. It is recorded that Rikyū was especially fond of using bamboo baskets for flowers in the tea ceremony (Ikeda 1980:219). His choice of containers was as innovative as his selection of tea utensils. He is said to have preferred everyday objects, such as a fish basket or the woven sheath for a woodcutter's hatchet. In them he placed flowers that looked as natural as if they were still in the wild. These baskets with their unpretentious arrangements must have been particularly harmonious in the setting of the *sōan*. They had a significant impact both on the art of flower arrangement (Ōi 1964:90-94) and on the style of basketry. The artful plucking and placing of a few flowers in a natural way for *chanoyu* came to be known as *chabana* (lit., "tea flowers"), as distinguished from the more elaborate art of arrangement now called *ikebana*. The style of simple and distinctly Japanese baskets employed by Rikyū, and associated with *chanoyu*, is now known as *wagumi*.

Long after Rikyū's death, rustic baskets retained their popularity. Many were either commissioned or made by tea masters themselves. One particularly famous and widely-copied basket was made by Hisada Sōzen (1647-1707), an active tea master during the Edo period (Ikeda 1980:241). This kind of basket, named Sōzen Kago after its creator, has a very stable, balanced form with a square bottom, a round rim, and usually a handle (Pl. 9). In the *tokonoma* of a tea ceremony room, its stability strongly underlines the beauty of the flowers, and its simplicity

complements all kinds of tea utensils (Fig. 3).

Wagumi basketry is fashioned with much wider, coarser bamboo strips than *karamono*, and has a relaxed, spontaneous feeling. Symmetry is not essential; in fact sometimes there are intentional irregularities. Compared to the eloquently refined Chinese style, *wagumi* has a warm, earthy quality. Ikeda Hyōa, who specializes in baskets for *chanoyu* (see Fig. 2), said: "I try to make a basket with a soft feeling. Flowers used for tea ceremony do not look good in a hard, precisely crafted basket. If a basket is made in complete perfection it does not have a place for the beauty of flowers." Hyōa also explained that in *chanoyu*, baskets are used only during the warmer months from April or May to October, when water is boiled on the portable brazier (*furo*) instead of the winter fire pit (*ro*). During the colder months ceramic vases and bamboo tube containers are used for display. As a rule, baskets are arranged not with flowers from trees, but only with those from the ground, which are abundant in the warmer season. With them, Hyōa feels, a flower basket made from organic material like bamboo is especially harmonious and brings a cool airy atmosphere into the tea room during the warmer months.

The Tea Ceremony with *Sencha*

The *senchadō* evolved in the seventeenth century during the early Edo period. Japan had closed its doors to all foreign countries except Holland and China; trade with these nations was

carried out under the supervision of a governmental agency at Nagasaki in Kyushu. The literati of that era wished to liberate themselves from the closed system of feudalistic Edo society. To them it seemed that the highly formalized *chanoyu* had lost its previous spirituality and creativity. They took as their models the intelligentsia of the Chinese Ming dynasty, who at that time were drinking brewed green-leaf tea, or *sencha*. For the literati, this was more than merely a new, exotic type of tea. Drinking it was noble, and constituted a new way of life. Thus they devoted themselves to *senchadō*, the "way of *sencha*." Sometimes they would congregate at each other's homes for tea drinking and cultured conversation. Often they would choose beautiful sites, at the riverside or in the mountains for example—settings of nature which they admired and glorified in poetry and painting. As the fashion took hold, the drinking of *sencha*, which began in a sense as a turning away from rigid ritual, became ceremonialized. Since *chanoyu* was never eclipsed, the two tea ceremonies in effect coexisted. But throughout the Edo period the *sencha* ceremony was an important part of the literati movement which had such significance for Japanese culture, and out of which so many famous painters and writers emerged.

Many of the utensils used in the *sencha* ceremony were made from bamboo, which was thought to possess virtues such as spiritual nobility and cleanliness. Ogawa suggests that the literati identified bamboo with the virtues they themselves were pursuing (1986:102-103). The artists who were interviewed all agreed on the importance of the *sencha* movement in the development of bamboo baskets, which were and still are very popular as flower containers for the *sencha* ceremony. The *tokonoma* of a *senchadō* room is typically adorned with a hanging scroll, an incense burner and holder, and flowers arranged in a bamboo basket. Whereas for *chanoyu* the bamboo basket is only used during the warmer months, for the *sencha* ceremony it is utilized all year round.

Since the *sencha* movement sprang from an admiration and yearning for the life style of the Chinese literati, imported baskets were once again much in demand, along with other Chinese objects. Japanese basket makers were asked to repair baskets that had been damaged during transport from the continent. According to Tanabe Shōchiku, those with a reputation for superior craftsmanship were invited to replicate *karamono*. Great numbers were copied—especially in the late nineteenth century, when *senchadō* reached its peak of popularity, and particularly in the Kansai region. At first basket makers tried to make very exact copies of the meticulous, elegant work. Gradually, however, their work began to express a distinct Japanese flavor. Unlike the *wagumi* baskets made for *chanoyu* discussed earlier, these did not show intentional asymmetry nor did they depart radically from Chinese type. Still basically in the style of *karamono*, they were nevertheless recognizably Japanese.

25

Figure 3. Tea ceremony utensils: cup, scoop, whisk, and lacquered tea-powder container. Courtesy of Sōsei Matsumoto. Los Angeles, May 1988.

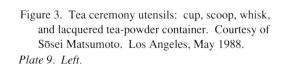

Plate 9. Left.

New Forms of Basketry and
The Signed Basket

The *sencha* ceremony, reflecting the ideology of the literati who sought spiritual freedom from authority and tradition, provided the milieu for greater freedom of expression and experimentation in art forms (Ogawa 1986:441). Floral arrangements were more varied and drew on a wider range of flowers in the *sencha* ceremony than in the older *chanoyu*. New forms of ornament also appeared in the *tokonoma*, such as colorful fruits of the season, attractively arranged in a kind of shallow basket known as *morikago* (Pls. 10,11).

Many new and highly creative forms of basketry emerged during this time. Basket makers also began to sign their works. According to Osabe et al. (1985:10), one of the first to do so consistently was Hayakawa Shōkosai I

安石全覺大谷
棃里夾路遠塵
相結甘酸白秘
丹青裡止渴群
程芳是准
淇園主人畫
旦題

Plate 10. Right.
Plate 11a,b. Above.

Plate 12.

Plate 13. Right.
Plate 14 a,b. Far right.

(1815-1897), great-grandfather of the contemporary Shōkosai V, who commented,

> *A new expression in bamboo baskets in Japan was a natural development since the quality of Chinese and Japanese bamboo is different. Although [my great-grandfather] depended on the style and technique of* karamono *baskets for his basic foundation, he also attempted to show his own aesthetic sensibility which could* *be expressed through Japanese bamboo, and thus he signed his works (see Pl. 12).*

The signing of a work marked an important transition in the development of bamboo basketry, since it reflected the consciousness of basket makers as individual artists who create their own art style rather than merely copying Chinese baskets (Osabe et al. 1985: 9,10).

The number of signed baskets increased espe-
cially in the Kansai region, where *senchadō* was so popular. There craftsmen began to produce pieces with distinctive personal styles. After Hayakawa Shōkosai I there were others, including his son Shōkosai III (1864-1922), Tanabe Chikuunsai I (1877-1937), and Maeda Chikuhōsai I (1872-1950), all famous for their artistry and excellent technique. Three baskets illustrated here show Chikuhōsai's mastery of diverse styles (Pls. 13,14). These artists were

known as well for their Japanese-style rough basket work. Nevertheless, Hayakawa Shōkosai V and Tanabe Shōchiku, both now active in the Kansai area, agreed:

> ...the bamboo basketry of this region has developed from karamono baskets of the sencha ceremony. This background is still a strong current in the tradition. Elegance and refinement are important qualities which a bamboo artist seeks in his works. This quality is also parallel with the highly cultivated taste of literati.

The baskets of the Kansai region display the distinctive characteristics that have developed from *karamono*, such as the use of very narrow bamboo strips, delicate, precise interworking, and decorative details around the rims and handles (Pls. 12,13). Even among the more roughly crafted baskets, the taste for elegance can be observed in details such as the handle attachments of Chikuhōsai's work (Pl. 14a).

Basketry
in the
Modern Era

In 1858, just ten years before the end of the Edo period, Japan officially opened itself to the outside world. During the Meiji period that followed, the new government encouraged trade in order to enrich the country. Tanabe Shōchiku explained that trade policies favored the export of a great number of bamboo baskets to foreign countries. To stimulate the growth of industry, including arts and crafts, the government held a periodic "Domestic Industrial Exposition." Many other public and private exhibitions were also organized. Basket makers displayed their work domestically and also sent it to international exhibitions. According to Moroyama and Kaneko in Osabe et al. (1985:140, 146-158), a few bamboo works were sent to the Vienna Exposition of 1873; and Hayakawa Shōkosai III—apparently a master at the age of fourteen—won a prize for his work at the Paris Exposition in 1878.

Other factors as well encouraged a substantial increase in production of bamboo baskets. The popularity of the *sencha* tea ceremony continued strongly from the Meiji period up until World War II. As Ōi has pointed out (1964:134-139), flower arrangement became very popular among middle class women as a sign of refinement. Naturally flower baskets were required for this activity. However it was above all the national and international exhibitions that played an important role in encouraging bamboo basket makers to develop a creative art form.

Bamboo Craft as a Creative Art Form

One of the most important leaders in the movement to raise bamboo craft to an art form was Iizuka Rōkansai (1880-1958). Rōkansai was active during the Taishō and early Shōwa periods, between 1912 and the 1950s, and had a profound influence on the modernization of bamboo craft (Osabe et al. 1985:10-12). His son Shōkansai commented:

When my father was young, he wanted to have a career in oil painting, as I also did at one stage of my life. He was not satisfied with the old, traditional forms expressed by bamboo, although he was born into the family of a basket maker. But once he decided to become a bamboo artist, he always attempted to create his own style and his own expression in bamboo. Most baskets were painted with lacquer at that time, but he made them with leached bamboo to show the beauty of the plain bamboo strips. Since then baskets with leached bamboo have become very popular.

Rōkansai crafted many elaborate baskets with careful and precise attention to detail, but his most interesting and ingenious works seem to have been produced from long, wide, leached bamboo strips roughly worked into a globular shape. According to Osabe et al. (1985:12), Rōkansai himself did not refer to this technique as *ami*, the usual term for the crafting of baskets and certain other handiwork. Instead he called

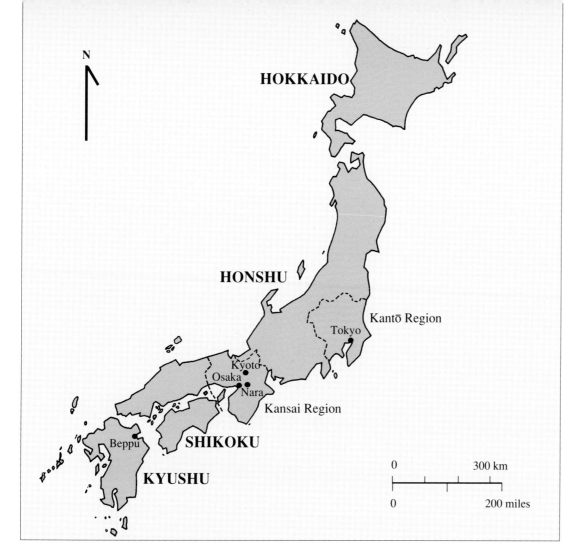

Figure 4. Map of Japan.

exhibit their best pieces in one of the annual shows. They plan carefully and work very hard to produce a basket that represents both mastery of technique and individual creativity. Informants agreed that summer is their busiest time, as the shows are usually held in the fall. While the majority of their works are flower baskets, they also make fruit baskets, trays, boxes, and other tea ceremony utensils such as whisks and scoops. Their pieces are signed, since they are, as Shōkansai said, "... the artist's own expression and we have a responsibility for our work."

Takekōgeika have not totally abandoned the role of craftsman. Though some may prefer creative work, if commissioned they will make a basket exactly as the customer desires, or copy a famous old piece impeccably, taking pride in superlative technique and artistic sensibility. Therefore their work really has two dimensions: one of creative basketry made for exhibitions, and the other of traditional forms made on commission.

Regional Differences in Basketry

It can be said that regional characteristics exist on a very general level (see map, Fig. 4). The source of the basketry tradition of the Kansai region is the *karamono* basket used in the *sencha* ceremony. Consequently Kansai baskets tend to be elaborately crafted of narrow strips, in a refined style. Even those less delicate baskets made with wider strips and irregular plaiting retain a sense of elegance. In the Kantō region,

 33

them *kumi,* "composition." Such pieces look more like sculpture than basketry. Rōkansai's influence was strong in the later development of bamboo basketry, and basket makers began to seek their own styles in the works they exhibited. The late Living National Treasure, Shōno Shōunsai (1904-1974), who was active in Kyushu, made a large number of lively, powerful pieces. His baskets show a high degree of refinement, and yet there remains the strength and

touch of wildness characteristic of traditional basketry in Kyushu.

Contemporary basket makers no longer identify themselves by the old-fashioned term *kagoshi* (lit., "basket maker"). Rather they are *takekōgeika* or *chikkōgeika,* "bamboo craft artists." Their work is more than artisanship. It is a new genre of art known—probably since shortly after World War II—as *takekōgei* or *chikkōgei* (lit., "bamboo craft art"). Many

Plate 15 a,b. *Left.*
Plate 16. *Above.*

where Iizuka Rōkansai led the radical modernization movement, basket styles are less traditional; forms and techniques are often innovative and experimental.

Kyushu has a fine reputation for its tradition of *kōkyū hanakago*, or "high-quality flower baskets"—a natural development since excellent bamboo grows there. Beppu, the renowned hot spring resort, is also the center of the local bamboo craft whose productivity was stimulated

by the policy of the Ōita Prefecture during the Taishō period (1912-1926), under which various styles and techniques were introduced into Beppu from the traditions of other regions. Flower baskets produced in Kyushu gradually developed a distinct style of their own. Their bamboo strips are wider than those of Kansai, and the manner of crafting is unrestrained and powerful. One notable technique is the insertion of short strips into the surface of the basket body to produce

straight vertical lines, *tatezashi* (Pl. 15) or a herringbone-like pattern, *yahazuzashi* (Pl. 16). Kyushu baskets may lack a high degree of refinement, but they have a rural vitality that avoids excessive detail.

However these regional differences should be thought of only in very broad terms. Many works in Kantō and Kyushu are very similar to those in Kansai, and of course by the same token, certain artists in Kansai and Kyushu are as innovative as

35

those in Kantō. It has been observed that since the interaction between bamboo artists from all regions has increased dramatically, and since their works are all exhibited in the same shows, regional differences are disappearing.

What the Artists Value

The artists who were interviewed have strong ideas about the ideal qualities of a flower basket. Iizuka Shōkansai strives to integrate both aesthetic beauty and function in his work and believes it is important to avoid excessive concern for technique, because an overworked basket becomes rather busy. When planning a basket, he always carefully considers the place and occasion of its use as well as its form, and tries to achieve a balance between the two. Function is a very important issue for him:

When I was young, the tendency was to consider function as of secondary importance to the aesthetic dimension. Some pieces became very abstract. I was also involved in this movement and experimented with various new forms. These unusual works naturally caught people's attention, but one tires of looking at them after a while. I feel that there is a range of expression for each material and this is true for bamboo as well. Besides, in the field of kōgei *["craft art"], function is a very important aspect which we cannot ignore. Of course it is appropriate to use a traditional material like bamboo for creative expression*

in the area of pure art. However, if we are to preserve traditional kōgei, *we should not forget function.*

Ikeda Hyōa emphasizes that a basket should give life to the flowers. The flowers should be the focus of attention and the basket should enhance their beauty. Apart from that, he feels that there is no standard by which its quality can be judged. It is simply a matter of taste. For example, although very decorative baskets are often disliked, they may look attractive with a showy flower arrangement in a big Western-style room. Moving from the aesthetic to the practical, he suggests that since the bottom of the basket is most frequently damaged, we should check that area carefully to see that it is sturdy.

Hayakawa Shōkosai explained his concept of a good basket by using two words: *shigoto* ("labor") and *saiku* (lit., "handiwork," but also "manipulation, trick"). Clearly Shōkosai intended the second meaning:

We can do as much shigoto *as we want in basket making. If we do honest* shigoto, *human nature and the spiritual part of the* takekōgeika *will be naturally reflected. It is not calculation. Those characteristics become the inherent value of the basket. However* saiku *is too intentional and self-conscious. There is too much showing off by the maker, as though he is indicating how hard he is trying. In this case a basket often ends up with an abundance of unnecessary decoration.*

The quality and characteristics of material are ignored, and thus the natural beauty of bamboo is destroyed. It is very difficult to know when to leave certain things out, but very important. On the other hand, I feel that basket makers should experiment when they are young. Through this process, one learns what to exclude. When I was young, I tried to conquer bamboo, but now I do my work by talking with the bamboo. I try to integrate its natural beauty with my designs. A good basket for me is one that has a natural feeling and shows the true beauty of bamboo without garish decoration. A basket with these qualities seems never to lose its freshness and to have a continual appeal.

Tanabe Shōchiku also emphasized that a good basket is one that expresses the natural beauty of bamboo. He thinks baskets conveying the personality and originality of the maker will retain their appeal in virtually any context. Moreover those works communicate something because they reflect the inner feeling of the artist.

The Training of a Bamboo Artist

Although there are some who learn the art of bamboo craft without benefit of family tradition, the majority have inherited it. Traditionally it has been a male occupation, but a few women are beginning to emerge as basket makers. All the artists interviewed were born into families specializing in the craft and thus were trained mainly by their fathers. What follows are personal accounts of their training, as recorded in September 1987.

Iizuka Shōkansai

"I am the third-generation bamboo artist in my family. When I was young I intended to become an oil painter so I entered the Tokyo School of Fine Arts and studied Western-style painting. However my elder brother, who was supposed to take over the family tradition, had poor health and died young. That was just after World War II, when I came back from military service. It was an extremely difficult decision for me to give up oil painting and begin to learn bamboo basket making. Although I had helped to make baskets from my childhood, the art form always seemed too old-fashioned and stale for me. Instead I thought I could express myself much more freely in the area of oil painting. I also worried that I could not make a living from *takekōgei* during the chaotic period after the war. However there was no real choice except to carry

Figure 5. Iizuka Shōkansai selects a piece of leached bamboo. September 1987.

on the family tradition. My family had a very difficult time then. In addition to my brother's early death, my father had no apprentices because they had all gone to the war, so I did all of the assistant work. It was a difficult, frustrating job at the beginning. You need great patience to learn how to prepare bamboo, since it often splits in an unintended way or the strips break. It is very important to master the preparation of the material at the start of your career. And yet it is also worthwhile to try making a basket while you are learning the most basic preparation technique. Unless you do that, you will never understand the relationship between certain basketry methods and the type of bamboo strips used" (Fig. 5).

"My father was an old-fashioned man. He just said, 'Sit there and watch me.' He did not explain things to me nor show me how to do them by guiding my hands with his. I just watched what he was doing. After two years of training I was permitted to make my own basket. My father looked at my first work for a while, then jumped up and stamped on my basket. It was broken flat. He did not say a word about the basket, but ordered me to make another one. I was very upset since I had confidence in my first work and did not understand what was wrong with it. On other occasions my baskets were cut into pieces with scissors or thrown into the hearth by my father. At that time I did not understand why he did those things. I frequently thought I would give up this activity, since I had a lingering attachment to oil painting. Mortification at my father's assessment of my work and determination to make a basket that would satisfy him motivated me to continue working.

"Now I often think about my father's action. My formal art education at the art school may have hindered me in the training process. Perhaps I tried to show off my knowledge of art forms when I was still not ready. My father tried to get me to recognize that I would never mature unless I humbly started afresh and tried to develop the mind of an artisan who respects the necessity of precise technique. Maybe that is why his way of teaching was so harsh. Since he never taught me by words, I always tried to think and discover what he wanted me to learn. When rejected my work, I would reflect on it very carefully to determine what I had done wrong. The next time, when I changed my work and my father approved it, I would know that my assessment was correct. Thus my training was very slow, but the things that I learned in this way seem to have been internalized quite well.

"Usually it takes about ten years to master *takekōgei*. It is a very complicated form of craft because the student has to master the precise details of bamboo splitting, stripping, polishing, and 'weaving'. We also learn how to care for the various tools of a basket maker" (Figs 6,7). "We have to know the specific way to prepare bamboo into appropriate strips for certain 'weaves'. When we accumulate all of this knowledge and technical skill, and when we can successfully express our own art in a bamboo basket by applying what we have learned, we will be recognized as an independent *takekōgeika*. After this, one tries to produce baskets expressing one's own aesthetic sense, and attempts to have them shown in an exhibition. One will establish a reputation as an artist through the process of being accepted into these shows, or, if fortunate, by receiving a prize.

"I am teaching several people now, but none of them live in my house. It is very difficult to find such apprentices today. Modern young people do not want to put themselves into that situation. I myself believe that a traditional apprenticeship, living in the teacher's household, is extremely valuable, because the student can then learn the spiritual and moral dimensions of the art. Young people may think it is a waste of time to clean the teacher's garden or studio, as traditional apprentices did, but I believe that the character traits required to patiently clean these places are closely related to those qualities of mind necessary to the achievement of a high level of technique as a bamboo artist.

"I accept as a student anyone who has a strong motivation to master this craft art. This, I believe, is the most critical factor in order to survive the difficult training process. More important than talent is the student's determination to continue. If you stick to one thing and try very hard to master it, you will eventually succeed. The ideal time to start is probably after graduating from high school [because] I believe in the lifelong importance of basic education. I always tell the beginner that it will take about ten years to become independent. Often people have a difficult time after about four years of study. It may be coincidental that recently two of my students quit training after four years, but four years is too short a period really to master *takekōgei*. Former students who have become independent occasionally visit me. They come to ask my opinion about their plans for new pieces, or about the pieces themselves. I often give them my advice before they send their work to exhibitions.

"We may now need a formal education system for *kōgei*. That way we could teach the techniques and also develop the aesthetic sensibilities of the students. If this is not done, young people today may not follow this tradition anymore. From my experience it was an extremely slow process to learn because my father did not teach me through verbal explanations. Thus I feel that it is necessary to teach systematically, perhaps also adding a scientific dimension. Describing precisely how to handle a saw and where to cut the bamboo, and then explaining the reason why we do it that way may be a useful method. Students may learn much faster. But I suspect that some people who go through this training process may fail after they graduate. The techniques they learned in class may soon be forgotten or decline in quality because their knowledge and practice are primarily theoretical rather than something truly internalized through experience. However I also believe that some people who have strong motivation recognize the shortcomings of their technique and the weak quality of their work, and thus still practice and polish their skill after graduation. These people may eventually succeed as very good bamboo artists."

When I asked Shōkansai about what aspects he specially emphasized in his teaching, he answered the question by first describing three categories of craft. "Although the general public does not distinguish the differences, they have been clearly separated since the last war. The first category consists of those objects which can be mass-produced and are inexpensive. The second is that of folk art, primarily ordinary utensils. These should be suitable for everyday use and thus should be strong. The third is craft art (*kōgei*), which emphasizes the aesthetic as well as the functional.

"This classification of craft is not meant to be hierarchical, since the purposes of each group are different. *Takekōgei* has function as its basis, but it is also essential that we communicate our own ideas and aesthetic sense in our work. So I think that it is very important to develop a sensibility for beauty. I did my copies of fine old baskets. I had an opportunity to study the famous baskets in the Shōsōin and thereby gained considerable knowledge about ancient baskets. It is important for the artist to look at all art forms, such as painting and calligraphy, and internalize them. This knowledge and sensitivity for art will eventually be expressed in our work as our own art style. When one becomes an independent bamboo artist, it does not mean that one's training has finished. We still need to be open and receptive to all forms of art in order to grow. It is a lifelong process."

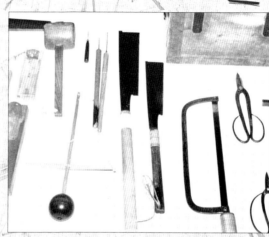

Figure 6. Iizuka Shōkansai's tool table has an array of knives and saws. A basket maker must learn to use and care for a great variety of tools.

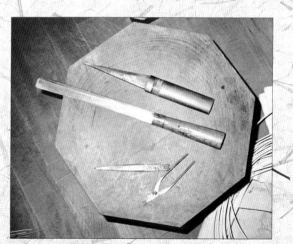

Figure 7. Iizuka Shōkansai's cutting board with two knives. September 1987.

39

Ikeda Hyōa

"I learned basket making from my father. Since the tradition of my family is to make bamboo baskets for *chanoyu*, it is essential to understand its rules and artistic taste. The ceremony has a tradition of about 500 years, and consequently the art works used in it should be expressive of the aesthetic taste that has evolved in the course of this long history. So my training in basket making proceeded parallel with the study of tea ceremony. I started making simple baskets when I was 15 or 16 years old. After my father died, when I was 19, I had to learn by myself. My main training consisted of careful observation and the study of old baskets preserved in the tea ceremony world. One of the top people in Japanese business circles sponsored me and gave me the precious opportunity to see many valued baskets which are kept in private collections. I did many copies of old masterpieces. I started producing my own creative work when I joined the Association of Traditional Craft Art.

"In *takekōgei* it is essential to learn how to prepare the materials skillfully as well as to study various basket making techniques, but in addition to these technical aspects, one must develop one's artistic sensibility. We need to look carefully at old baskets in order to gain that sense. I would like to emphasize the art appreciation process in the training of bamboo basket makers.

"At the beginning it is difficult to manipulate the bamboo strips without their breaking. However it is perhaps even harder to produce the final version of a basket at exactly the size that has been planned. It is extremely difficult to bend the strips in precisely the desired form at the base zone between the bottom and body of the basket. In this area one often fails to achieve the original plan. It took a long time for me really to master this part of the work. Although I personally believe that there is no end to training, a person is generally recognized as an independent bamboo artist when his work is accepted in exhibitions or has won a prize. In the Japanese art world one has to be accepted and gain prizes in public exhibitions in order to make a professional career as an artist."

40

Hayakawa Shōkosai

"My formal training in *takekōgei* started when I was 19, after I graduated from high school. The teacher was my father. In our family we do not take any apprentices from outside. The father trains the eldest son and hands down all of his knowledge and technique to him. Each generation retains the name of Shōkosai. This custom is called *isshi sōden* in Japan. The training was very strict. My family possesses a special technique of scraping bamboo strips with a sharp knife. It takes a much longer time and is harder work to prepare bamboo materials in this way than by the ordinary technique, but the strips have an extremely even thickness and a pleasingly smooth surface with nice luster. It took me three to four years to master this technique alone. I had to continue scraping day after day until my father was satisfied with my work. It was awfully boring to do the same thing over and over again, but I endured this tedious labor with the hope that I would learn to make baskets someday. When my father finally recognized my accomplishment in the bamboo scraping technique, I was allowed to begin learning the basic techniques such as square, hexagonal, and twill plaiting. At the beginning, the result of our failures is that we frequently cut our hands. I still do that on occasions. I think that it is very important to copy old baskets—especially those with very fine, detailed structures, such as *karamono* pieces. You can achieve a delicate, precise workmanship by doing so. The best time to do this is when you are young, with good eyes and vigor.

"Our family has one tradition similar to a graduation exam, which determines if the son has mastered all of the technique of basket making. We have three totally different baskets and the candidate has to make copies exactly like them. The three originals contain every kind of basket work, and a combination of straight and curved lines, which a person who will eventually inherit the name Shōkosai must master. Even though I passed this examination, I was never sure my father recognized me as an independent artist" (Fig. 8). "I myself think that my training will not end until my last day. There is an old Japanese saying, 'ten years for splitting bamboo'. The literal meaning is that it takes ten years to master bamboo splitting. But I also take it to mean that it is very important to spend enough time and energy preparing the material."

Figure 8. A contemporary basket by Hayakawa Shōkosai. September 1987.

41

Tanabe Shōchiku

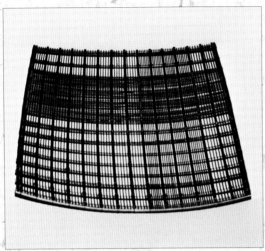

Figure 9. A contemporary basket by
Tanabe Shōchiku. September 1987.

"I have been fond of painting and craft work since I was a small child. During the last war, elementary school pupils who lived in big cities were evacuated to the countryside. My group went to a village where a lot of bamboo grew. Since we did not have any toys, we made things to play with out of bamboo, such as stilts and dragonflies. Also as a child I always saw my father making bamboo baskets." (His father is the famous Tanabe Chikuunsai. Tanabe Shōchiku will inherit his father's name.)

"While I was growing up, it was only natural for me to enter into this world. My formal training started when I graduated from high school, although I also studied *kōgei* at an art college in Tokyo. In the beginning I started to learn how to split bamboo and then I began to 'weave'. Although my father was my main teacher, two senior apprentices also gave me instruction. There was not much hardship for me during the training period, since I got into this world because I liked it. The most worthwhile aspect of my training was to copy baskets made by my elders, including my grandfather, my father, and their students. In copying the baskets of other people, I began to understand what concepts led to the production of a certain shape or 'weave'. I think it takes about ten years to become an independent bamboo artist. From about the time one has achieved independence one begins to send work to public exhibitions. If the works are selected for the shows and win prizes, one gradually establishes a reputation. Thus it is very important to exhibit your works in public. I know a person who has splendid talent and skill in making bamboo baskets, but he never sends his work to shows, so nobody knows his name. It is a waste that someone like him is just forgotten and his works unrecognized.

"I have fifteen students now, including eight female students. They do not live in my house, but come to study. I encourage my students to express their own creativity. At the beginning of training it is very important to master precise technique. I want them to be artisans at first, but gradually I try to encourage them to be artists who can communicate their own personality and feeling in their work" (Fig. 9).

The Making of Bamboo Baskets

Bamboo is the principal material used in the making of flower baskets. Other materials, such as rattan, wisteria vine, *akebi* vine, tree roots, and the bark of Japanese cypress are employed for specific purposes. Rattan, which has a beautiful luster and extreme flexibility, is often utilized for the particularly delicate parts of the basket such as the wrapping of the rim or handle, or for elaborate knots and stitches. In the Meiji and Taishō periods (A.D. 1868-1912, 1912-1926), bamboo rhizome and tree roots were frequently used, especially for the handle, because their complicated, crooked shapes provided a distinctive accent to the basket. However this fashion is rarely seen today.

Bamboo

There are fourteen genuses and more than six hundred species of what is generally referred to as bamboo (*take*) and bamboo grass (*sasa*) in Japan (Satō 1974:4). The first grows well in warmer climates, the second in cooler ones. Kyushu is famous for its large groves of *take*, as earlier noted. There is not much *take* on Hokkaido, but large areas of this northern island are covered with *sasa*. Bamboo must have begun to grow sometime during the Jōmon period, when the climate became warmer after the Pleistocene age. Although some species have been brought from China, many seem to be indigenous to Japan. The commonest kind, known as *madake* (*Phyllostachys bambusoides*), is believed to be indigenous (Ueda 1979:15-16). It is also used

most often in basketry. It has a solid, firm texture, with great flexibility, and can be readily split into straight strips. This quality is extremely important because basket makers frequently cut it into very fine strips—at times as small as 1.5-2 millimeters in width. Other varieties used for baskets include *suzutake* (*Bambusa brealis*), *nemagaridake* (*Sasa kurilensis*), *medake* (*Arundinaria simonii*), and *hachiku* (*Phyllostachy nigra*). Some types of *hachiku* change color in autumn, turning blackish violet. Another type of the same species develops dark spots on its body; the late Living National Treasure, Shōno Shōunsai, often used it for his work.

According to Sagami Akira, owner of a bamboo store in Kyoto, the best season for harvesting is the late autumn. Bamboo cut at this time of year is much less likely to have insects nesting in the interior. In this he agrees with Satō, who notes that bamboo cut during these months has a firm fiber which is very suitable for craft work. Furthermore the liquid content of bamboo decreases by about 50-60 percent around this time, substantially lowering the chance of mildew (Satō 1974:29). Sagami prefers to cut three- to four-year-old bamboo, since while it has grown to a reasonable extent it is not yet old, and has the proper degree of firmness and flexibility. After cutting, the bamboo is washed with water and scraped in order to remove dirt and a white, powder-like substance that some species produce on their surface. Sagami mixes rice chaff with the water to facilitate the cleaning, while others

Plate 17 .

use cordage to scrub the surface. The cleaned bamboo is arranged in a vertical position in a shady, well-ventilated place for several months to complete the drying process prior to leaching.

Leached Bamboo Normally the bamboo used for basketry goes through a process whereby the oil is leached out from its body; such bamboo is termed *sarashidake*. This results in a clean, yellowish-white surface tone and increases its luster (Pl. 17). It also enhances the flexibility and firmness of the fibers and provides additional protection against insect and mildew damage. When bamboo is to be dyed, this is absolutely essential. There are two leaching methods. The traditional way is to heat the bamboo repeatedly over a charcoal fire. (Today a gas fire is some-times used.) The second method is much less expensive, especially since many pieces can be treated at once. The bamboo is boiled in an alkaline solution, after which it is dried under the sun for about two weeks. Because this drying process further bleaches out the color, individual pieces have to be rotated so that all sides achieve the same tone. Sagami asserted that the tradi-tional method, although it has the disadvantage of being expensive and time consuming, produces a superior quality of *sarashidake*. Bamboo boiled in the alkaline solution tends to crack easily; and because it contains alkaline there is a possibility that it will turn a darker color when wet.

Sooted Bamboo No matter what its species, any bamboo that has been used as part of the framing of a traditional Japanese thatched roof house is called *susutake*. As a result of exposure for decades to the soot produced by the cooking or hearth smoke, it turns to a dark reddish-brown color (Pl. 18). An especially deep, rich color suffuses the entire body of pieces over a hundred years old. However very old sooted bamboo sometimes loses its flexibility, which is a disadvantage for basket making. *Susutake* is highly prized by basket makers because of its beautiful color. Sagami pointed out that it shows subtle differences of hue depending on the types of fuel burned in various regions. Straw, for example, produces a lighter hue, and wood a darker one. During the last several decades, according to Ikeda Hyōa, a great number of traditional houses have been demolished to be replaced by modern structures in the Tokyo region; consequently there has been a substantial supply of sooted bamboo. But these old houses are disappearing rapidly, so it will be increasingly difficult to obtain this material in the future. Although attempts have been made to produce the color of *susutake* artificially, thus far the results lack the depth and delicacy of the bamboo that has gone through the long natural process.

Artists usually purchase their material from bamboo stores and then split it themselves to the desired size. When I asked the craftsmen what characteristics they were looking for in the bamboo, they generally emphasized that the fiber should be firm and flexible, but pointed out that

Plate 18.

their selection depends a great deal on the type of basket to be made. It is very important to choose straight pieces that do not have prominent knots, for the fiber around knots is the most complicated part of the bamboo, and very difficult to split or cut properly.

Preparing the Bamboo

All of the bamboo artists interviewed emphasized the importance of the preparation process. It is essential that the bamboo strips be well split with a uniform width, and they must be smoothed and carefully scraped to an even thickness. This is very time consuming, and requires great patience and skill. Hayakawa Shōkosai, who demonstrated how to split and scrape bamboo, said that the preparation sometimes takes much more time than actual crafting of the basket.

Initial Cutting and Scraping First, the bamboo is cut to the desired length with a special saw (Fig. 10). If the strips are to be dyed later, the exterior skin of the leached bamboo has to be scraped off, since it contains large amounts of wax and silica which would prevent successful dyeing (Satō 1974:45). It is very important to scrape without making any deep scratches so that the surface will be as even and smooth as possible (Fig. 11).

Splitting After being scraped, the bamboo is split (*wari*) in half. Characteristically, it splits straight along its fiber. The knife should be

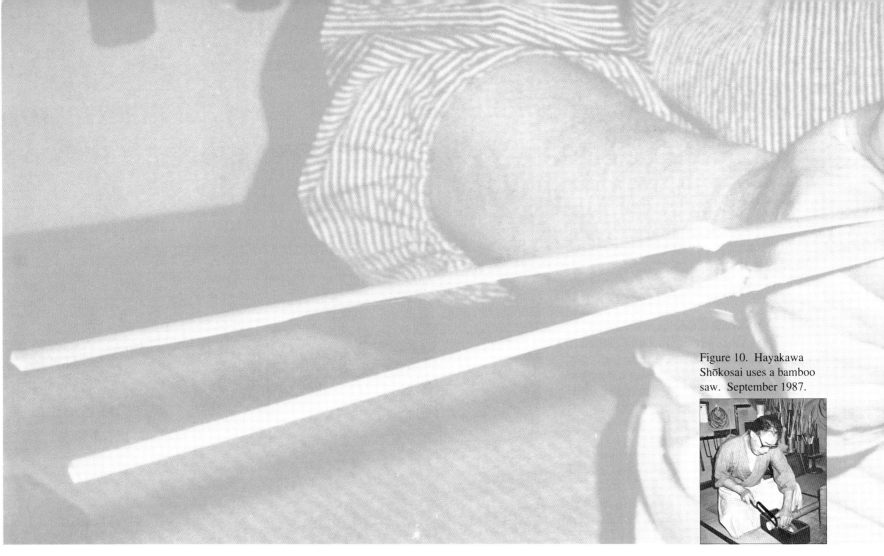

Figure 10. Hayakawa Shōkosai uses a bamboo saw. September 1987.

placed so that it will cut precisely along the diameter. The direction of splitting is usually from the upper stalk toward the root end (Fig. 12) because this way it splits more easily than the other way around (Satō 1974:48). Hayakawa Shōkosai then uses a measuring instrument to indicate where the next cuts will be made. The piece of bamboo is repeatedly split in half until the desired width is achieved (Fig. 13).

Stripping After the bamboo is split it must be stripped (*hagi*, *hegi*), which can be done by one of two methods. The first, called *hirahagi* (Fig. 14a), involves stripping the outer surface and the inner soft part with the same knife used for the prior splitting (Fig. 15). Shōkosai then uses a smaller knife to shave off the irregular edges of knots, and further scrapes the inner side of the *hirahagi* strip until it is smooth and has attained an even thickness (Fig. 16). The shiny

surface of the bamboo is used as the outer part of the basket. Ordinarily these are the kind of strips used for bamboo baskets and almost all utilitarian containers.

By the second method, called *masawari* (Fig. 14b), a strip of bamboo is further split laterally into finer pieces, sometimes as narrow as 1.5 millimeters. In this case the surface of the basket shows the split strips in cross section along the radius rather than along the circum-

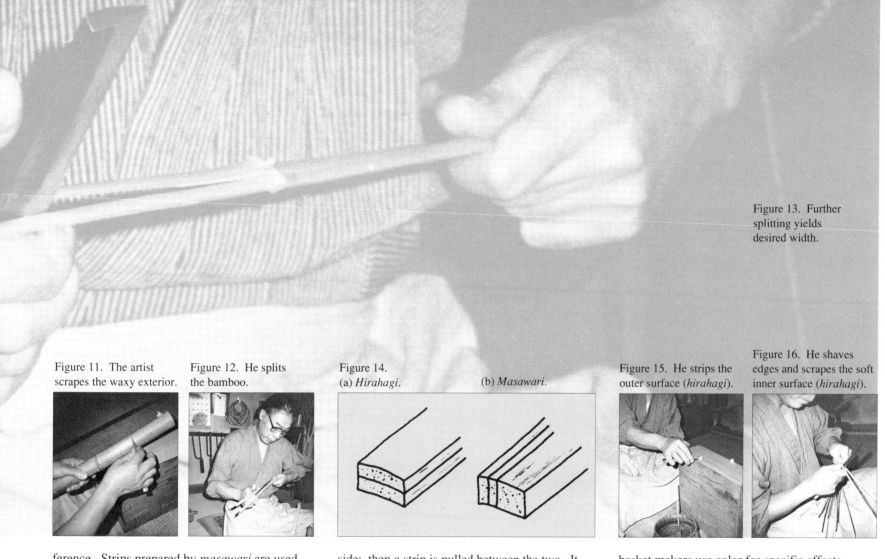

Figure 13. Further splitting yields desired width.

Figure 11. The artist scrapes the waxy exterior.

Figure 12. He splits the bamboo.

Figure 14.
(a) *Hirahagi*.

(b) *Masawari*.

Figure 15. He strips the outer surface (*hirahagi*).

Figure 16. He shaves edges and scrapes the soft inner surface (*hirahagi*).

ference. Strips prepared by *masawari* are used for special techniques in fancy flower baskets. For example, Iizuka Shōkansai favors one called *tabane-ami*, in which as many as twenty strips are plaited in bundles.

Cutting the widths The last step of preparation before dyeing is to cut the strips into the desired width. A pair of small, sharp knives are attached firmly to a cutting board, one for each

side; then a strip is pulled between the two. It requires great skill to pull evenly so that the cut edges are parallel to the natural lines of the bamboo fiber. Since the edges are very sharp and dangerous at this stage, they must be gently scraped and smoothed with a knife.

Dyeing and Coloring While many baskets are made of leached bamboo, which displays the clean, fresh beauty of the material itself, all

basket makers use color for specific effects. Sometimes they choose *susutake*, already colored naturally by its long exposure to smoke. Usually, however, they dye their bamboo strips prior to starting the handiwork. (Although a finished basket can be dipped in dye, its under parts will be much lighter in color than its surface.) The strips to be dyed should be leached and the outer skin scraped off. This is most commonly done with a basic commercial, chemical dye, especially the color called Bismarck Brown, which has the advantage of being able to penetrate well through the hard outer fiber and into the body of the bamboo.

Each artist tends to have a preferred way of coloring. Ikeda Hyōa and Tanabe Shōchiku often apply lacquer to the surface by rubbing it on with a cloth. This not only gives an elegant dark shade and luster, but also solidifies the texture and structure of the basket. Tanabe Shōchiku also uses another method which involves repeatedly heating a whole narrow bamboo tube over a fire until it achieves a rich dark brown.

Hayakawa Shōkosai's special dyeing technique has been passed down in his family tradition. An old plum tree is cut into small pieces and boiled for about twenty-four hours until it yields a dark brown liquid. For as long as it takes to achieve the desired tone, the bamboo strips are dipped in the plumwood extract, which imparts a soft, appealing color characteristic of plant dyes. The dyed strips are then polished with oil extracted from camellia to enhance their luster. According to Shōkosai, there is a chemical in plum wood that protects against insect damage. The variety with red blossoms produces a particularly refined color, but is very difficult to find. Though his plum tree dye method is extremely costly and time consuming, Shōkosai would like to pass it on to the next generation. But since this may not be possible, he hopes to develop a new technique appropriate to present circumstances and still to carry on, to some extent, his family tradition.

48

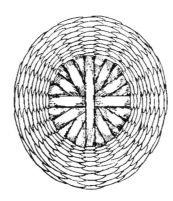
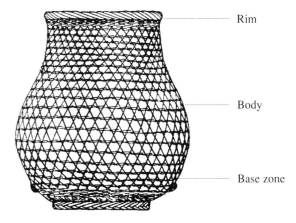

Figure 17. (a) Bottom, left.
(b) Base zone, body, and rim, above.

Crafting the Basket

Ami is the general Japanese term for the process used in making traditional handicrafts such as mats, nets, and baskets. It also describes "modern" handiwork such as lace and shawls, borrowed from the West. It can variously mean plaiting (or plaited), twining (or twined), netting, matting, braiding, twisting, knitting, crocheting, or the interlacing of elements. Since *ami* has no precise equivalent in English, it is often loosely translated as "weaving," "weave," or "woven"; however it should be understood that the term *ami* is never used with reference to the weaving of cloth. Such a translation is used here only when there seems no satisfactory alternative, and with the caveat that it is not a technical description, but rather a general term of convenience: for baskets, whether in fact plaited or twined, are popularly perceived to be "woven."

There are a tremendous number of basket making techniques in Japan, and their names differ regionally. The terms used here are the ones given in Osabe et al. (1985). Sometime in the 1960s these terms were standardized by common consent of the bamboo artists. English equivalents are taken mostly from Adovasio's *Basketry Technology* (1977), which contains thorough descriptions of American Indian basketry. However, Japanese artists use many techniques not mentioned in Adovasio; for these, suitable translations have been provided. For crafting purposes, a basket is broadly divided into four main parts, here called bottom, base zone, body, and rim (Fig. 17a, b). A flower basket often has a high base and a handle as well. Each of these parts has its own requirements.

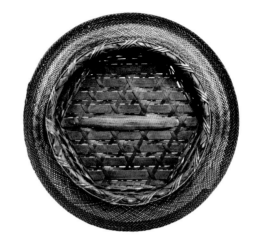

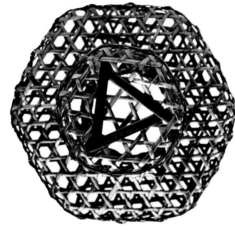

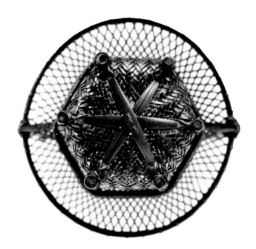

Left to right, top to bottom:
Figure 18. Basket bottom in square or four-mesh
  plaiting or *yotsume-ami* (basket, Plate 19).
Figure 19. Basket bottom in hexagonal or six-mesh
  plaiting or *mutsume-ami* (basket, Plate 20).
  Note artist's signature on reinforcing bamboo.
Figure 20. Basket bottom in crysanthemum plaiting
  or *kiku-ami* (basket, Plate 15a).
Figure 21. Basket bottom in twill plaiting or *ajiro-ami*
  (basket, Plate 15a).
Figure 22. Raft bottom or *ikadazoko* (basket, Plate 11a).

The Bottom A basket is begun almost invariably from the bottom. The four processes most frequently used here are square or four-mesh plaiting, *yotsume-ami* (Fig. 18, Pl. 19); hexagonal or six-mesh plaiting, *mutsume-ami* (Fig. 19, Pl. 20); crysanthemum plaiting, *kiku-ami* (Fig. 20, Pl. 15a); and twill plaiting, *ajiro-ami* (Fig. 21, Pl. 22). Octagonal or eight-mesh plaiting (*yatsume-ami*) is less common. Hexagonal plaiting always leaves open areas between the plaited strips, and this is often the case with square plaiting as well. Thus thick, widely cut bamboo pieces (*haritake* or *chikaratake*) must be inserted to strengthen the bottom and prevent breakage. On a square-plaited bottom these reinforcing strips can be placed in a variety of ways, for example criss-crossed diagonally or on a horizontal-vertical axis. On a hexagonal-plaited bottom, three pieces are usually applied on the diagonal or in triangle form. In both cases, the strips can also be inserted so that they are parallel. This results what is known as the "raft" bottom, or *ikadazoko* (Fig. 22, Pl. 11a). *Haritake* is also sometimes applied to a twill-plaited bottom, but chrysanthemum plaiting does not need any. When a basket maker puts his signature on the work, he carves it on top of the reinforcing bamboo (Fig. 19, Pl. 20). If there is none (as on chrysanthemum plaiting), he carves it either on top of a well-exposed spoke, or on a

bamboo strip inserted expressly for the signature.

The Base Zone The base zone makes the transition from the bottom of a basket to its body. It is the most difficult area to shape and stabilize, since the artist must bend and interwork the bamboo strips simultaneously. Sometimes the strips are moistened for easier manipulation. Thicker, less flexible ones are warmed over a mild source of heat such as a candle, and gradu-

ally bent to the desired angle. When the bottom is square-, hexagonal-, or twill-plaited, the same technique can be continued from base to body. However, chrysanthemum plaiting is only used for the bottom. Often the bamboo strips brought up from the bottom serve only as the warp (vertical strips), so that horizontal strips must be added separately to form a weft. When the bottom is chrysanthemum-plaited, the weft strips begin at an appropriate place at the bottom

(Fig. 20, Pl. 15a). Sometimes, in order to stabilize the base zone, special square-cut strips are used as wefts. Strips of this type, being stronger than the flat warps, hold them firmly. Twining is often used at the base zone for the same reason.

From left to right: Plates 19, 20, 21, 22.

The Body It is here that basket makers can display their artistic abilities most effectively, combining 'weaves' and manipulating the tightness of wefts to produce diverse shapes. Since there are innumerable techniques, only the most basic are given here. They fall into two broad groups according to strip size. When the strips are the same width, the structure is called *tomokumimono*. This group includes square, hexagonal, octagonal, and twill plaiting.

For each technique there are a variety of applications. For example, a simple form of square plaiting is rarely used on the body of fine art baskets; instead, a lozenge pattern —one application of square plaiting—seems most common (Fig. 23, Pl. 23a). Hexagonal plaiting, very popular for both artistic and utility baskets, has also been developed into a wide variety of patterns. Strips may be wrapped, for instance, by other strips (Fig. 24, Pl. 23b). Sometimes one horizontal and two diagonal strips are added to the hexagonal plaiting; this results in the hemp leaf motif, or *asa-no-ha* (Fig. 25).

52

Twill plaiting has also been worked into many complex configurations by the manipulation of the intervals. In basic twill plaiting, one strip passes over two other sets (Fig. 26, Pl. 17) or over three (2/2 or 3/3, respectively). These pass-over movements are carefully calculated and the intervals are shifted to make interesting patterns (Pl. 23c). Strips of different colors can be used to obtain further distinctive geometric designs.

When warps and wefts are of different size,

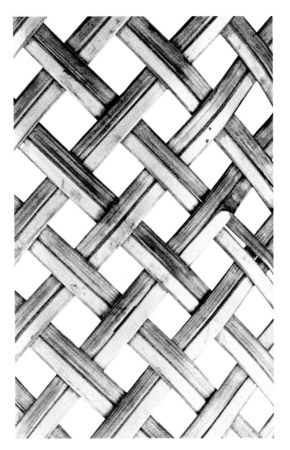

the structure is called *mawashimono*. Usually the warps are either wider than the wefts, or they are double instead of single. *Mawashimono* baskets are fashioned by one of two methods. The first is mat plaiting or *gozame-ami* (Fig. 27, Pl. 24a), which is uncomplicated and produces a sturdy piece; therefore everyday items such as kitchen baskets are usually made by this method. Its unpretentious beauty is also appreciated for artistic flower baskets. By this technique, a weft has to pass over and under the warp, alternating on each round. That is to say, if it goes over the warp on one register, it must go under on the next. This only works if there are an odd number of warps. Since each end of every bottom strip

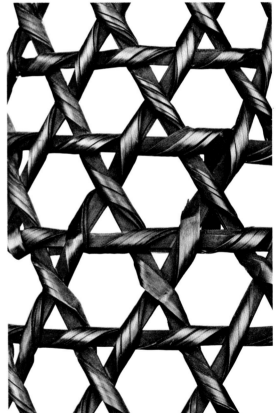

Figure 23. Lozenge pattern
(detail of Plate 23a). Left.
Figure 24. Wrapped hexagonal plaiting
(detail of Plate 23b). Above.

Clockwise from left:
Figure 25. Hemp leaf pattern, *asa-no-ha*.
Figure 26. Basic twill plaiting (detail of Plate 17).
Figure 27. Mat plaiting, *gozame-ami*
  (detail of Plate 24a).
Figure 28. Twining, *nawa-ami* (detail of Plate 24b).

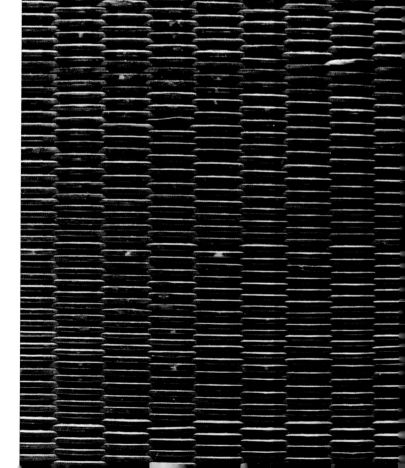

Plate 23 a,b,c. Above.
Plate 24 a,b. Far right.
Figure 29. Before bottom strips are turned upward, an extra strip must be added to ensure the uneven number of body warps required for mat plaiting.

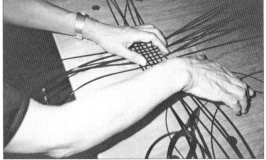

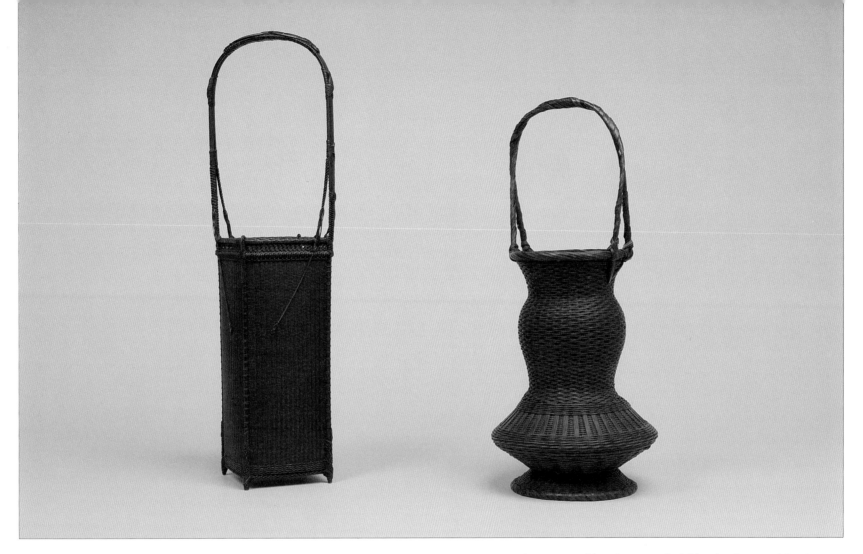

becomes a warp, there are always an even number of warp strips to begin with (Fig. 29). Therefore either an additional strip must be added at the bottom, or one of the strongest-looking warps must be split into two.

Twining, or *nawa-ami* (Fig. 28, Pl. 24b), is quite similar to mat plaiting, but in this case two or more wefts pass around the warps. In addition, the wefts themselves move up and down over one another. While the warps remain passive, the wefts move actively between the warps and among themselves in the same manner as seen in twine cordage (*nawa*). This technique is thus referred to as *nawa-ami*.

There are some baskets that cannot be classified as either *tomokumimono* or *mawashimono*. Some of the most popular flower baskets are made by an irregular plaiting technique called *midare*, in which many strips of bamboo are freely plaited and inserted into the body (Pl. 25).

Since hexagonal plaiting is often used for the base of this kind of basket, *midare* is sometimes classified as an application of hexagonal plaiting; but the end appearance of irregular plaiting is very different from that of hexagonal plaiting, which looks organized by comparison. Some of the artists mentioned that this technique is very challenging, since the basket maker must rely solely on his intuition to achieve a balanced, lively expression.

Plate 25. Above.
Detail, left.

Figure 30. Basic Body Techniques

Same-size warps & wefts [tomokumimono]	Warps wider than wefts [mawashimono]	Insertion [sashi]	Other
square plaiting [yotsume-ami] hexagonal plaiting [mutsume-ami] twill plaiting [ajiro-ami] octagonal plaiting [yatsume-ami]	mat plaiting [gozame-ami] twining [nawa-ami]	vertical insertion [tatezashi] herringbone insertion [yahazuzashi]	irregular plaiting [midare]

Two regular kinds of insertion (*sashi*) can be used to produce strong accents on the body of the basket: a vertical one called *tatezashi* (Pl. 26a) and another one called *yahazuzashi* (Pl. 16), so named because it resembles the tail of an arrow, *yahazu*, though to Western eyes it might be seen as a herringbone. The herringbone pattern can be oriented either vertically, from base to rim, or horizontally, to encircle the basket. A third technique involves inserting wide strips diagonally into the body (Pl. 27). Although this method is often classified as irregular plaiting, it seems more appropriate to categorize it as diagonal insertion, since its appearance is much more regular than that of irregular plaiting.

Moreover, in the latter, the strips are actually plaited, whereas in the former, the strips are only inserted into the body.

Some baskets have double walls (Pl. 28). At times this device is used so that the viewer can see both the interior and exterior patterns of the basket. It is also useful in supporting the outer wall when the basket work there is very complicated, as in Plate 29. The most basic types of technique are shown in Figure 30. From these many elaborate applications are developed.

Plate 26 a,b. Left.
Plate 27. Right.

60

Plate 28.

Plate 29.

The Rim Basket makers must keep in mind two important points when making the rim (*fuchi*). First, since it is the point of completion, its form has to be well balanced with the rest of the basket. Second, like the bottom, it is an area vulnerable to breakage. Thus strip ends must be carefully treated and sturdily wrapped. Rim techniques can be divided into three broad categories, *tomobuchi*, *makibuchi*, and *atebuchi*.

In *tomobuchi* the bamboo body strips are continued upward and manipulated to form the rim (Fig. 31, Pl. 27). Since this process requires a radical bending of the strips, there is a risk they will break—a terrible waste after one has labored on the whole body of the basket. To prevent this, each strip is moistened beforehand, or if thick, sliced into two pieces, increasing flexibility.

In *makibuchi* the ends of the interlaced strips are held in two bamboo cores, which are then wrapped continuously by strips prepared for rim work (Pl. 17). Usually the cores cannot be seen from the outside. This results in a very sturdy rim, so it is frequently used for utensils as well as for flower baskets. In *atebuchi* two or more wide bamboo strips encircle the rim to hold the ends of the body work. The exposed surfaces of the holding strips must be smooth and well prepared since they are a particularly conspicuous element of the basket. These strips are held together by

very narrow rattan strips, which are flexible
enough to bend into detailed forms. Often
the wrapping technique is quite elaborate
(Pls. 8b, 23c, 30a, 30b).

Figure 31. One type of *tomobuchi*, detail of Plate 27.

Plate 30 a,b,c.

Plate 31 a,b.

Figure 32. Simple wrapping (*bō-maki*),
   detail of Plate 21.
Figure 33. Wrapping with design (*sujiiri bō-maki*),
   detail of Plate 32.
Figure 34. Insect wrapping (*mushi-maki*),
   detail of Plate 23c.
Figure 35. Stitched insect wrapping (*kakemushi-maki*),
   detail of Plate 30b.
Figure 36. Cross knot (*jūji-musubi*).
Figure 37. Spiral cross knot (*jūji-uzumaki-musubi*),
   detail of Plate 23c.

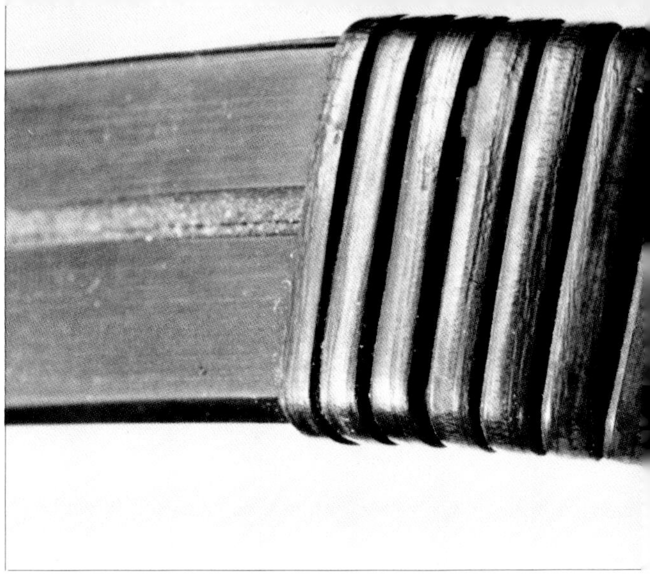

32.

33

Wrapping, Knots, and Stitches

It is not only at the rim that delicate rattan work can be observed. Rattan wrapping (*maki*), knots (*musubi*), and stitches (*tome* and *kagari*) are used to attach elements, hide undesirable features such as nails, or protect vulnerable areas such as the corners (Satō 1974:116). They also serve an important decorative function. Rattan work is most often seen on finely-wrought *karamono* baskets or those influenced by *karamono*; yet it is also evident on some of the more rough-hewn Japanese-style baskets, as can be seen in the work of Chikuhōsai (Pl. 14a). In other pieces by the same artist, elaborate rattan work becomes a very important decorative element in the overall design (Pl. 13). Wraps, knots, and stitches give a colorful accent to many of the other baskets shown here. These classical techniques have been incorporated with great enthusiasm into modern baskets; in fact it might be suggested they constitute one of the most important legacies of *karamono* basketry. Figures 32-43 illustrate twelve varieties of rattan work.

66

34.

35.

36.

37.

From left to right:
Figure 38. Interlocking 'V' knot (*kunoji-musubi*),
  detail of Plate 21.

68

Figure 39. Double interlocking 'V' knot,
  detail of Plate 23c.

Figure 40. Butterfly knot (*chō-musubi*),
  detail of Plate 11a.

Figure 41. Turtle-shell knot (*kame-no-ko-musubi*),
  detail of Plate 32.

Figure 42. Rice-character stitch (*kome-no-ji-dome*),
  replicating the character (borrowed from the Chinese)
  for rice, detail of Plate 22.

Figure 43. Insect stitch (*mushi-kagari*),
  detail of Plate 45c.

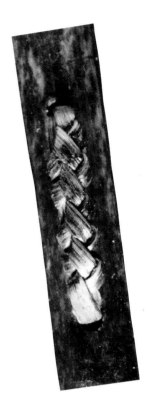

Containing Beauty

A basket maker spends many long days preparing bamboo strips for a new project. His attitude of uncompromising craftmanship, internalized during ten years of training, is the very foundation of his art. Japanese baskets reflect the rigor and devotion of the bamboo artists. Undoubtedly they themselves would wish us just to enjoy the baskets without imagining the tedium of their hard work. But if we understand what goes into their art our admiration can only deepen.

Japanese basketry owes much to the successive waves of influence from China, whose handiwork was borrowed time after time and then transformed into distinctly Japanese style. When Japan finally opened its doors to the larger world, it encountered Europe and found new inspiration. Inexorably Western civilization made its impact on the life of the people and their art forms.

Today Japanese households have grown very westernized. As the architecture changes, so do the crafts within. Many everyday utensils once made of bamboo have been replaced by synthetic objects. Since Second World War vases of all kinds have outnumbered baskets in department stores. Nevertheless most families still own baskets for *ikebana*, and the popularity of bamboo art seems to be on the rise again.

Traditionally the *tokonoma* provided a framework for the arrangment of art objects; at the same time it shaped and set limits to the forms of display. Now fewer and fewer houses have a *tokonoma*. The fact that most contemporary flower baskets are made without a handle may to some degree reflect this change. When a basket is placed in an alcove it is only seen from the front, and a handle is appropriate since it establishes frontality. But when the basket is taken out of that context, it can be viewed from all directions. In this case a handle may be seen as unnecessary or even as an encumbrance. Some people speak of liberation from the *tokonoma* and welcome its demise. Others are disturbed that people have begun to ignore the framework of the *tokonoma* and suggest that this will lead inevitably to the decline of traditional art forms.

The tradition is changing for other reasons, as well. Many young people are learning basketry outside of a family tradition. It has become popular among women; in fact some are gaining reputations as serious bamboo artists and have had their work selected for important exhibitions. This emerging class of practitioners will bring new perspectives to the ancient forms.

Artists who work in a craft tradition often face a paradoxical situation. They must at once preserve old forms and find new ones that express their own times. In a tradition as time-honored as flower basketry, it is a serious challenge. But there is no doubt that bamboo artists will find new ways of containing beauty.

71

Figure 44. Simple, flowing lines give this basket a modern flavor (see Plate 46).

72

Plate 32.

Plate 33 a,b,c.

Plate 34 a,b.

Plate 35 a,b,c.

Plate 36 a,b,c.

Plate 37 a,b.

78

Plate 40 a,b,c.

Plate 41 a,b.

Plate 42 a,b,c.

Plate 43 a,b.

Plate 44 a,b.

Plate 45 a,b,c.

Plate 46. *Above.*
Plate 47 a,b. *Right.*

Plate Captions

Plate 1. *The people of Tōkaidō (Jinbutsu Tōkaidō), Hamamatsu.* Color woodcut. 24.7 x 24.9 cm. Artist: Andō Hiroshige (1797-1858). During the early Edo period, the Tōkaidō, an ancient highway between Edo (Tokyo) and Kyoto, was equipped with travelers' facilities at 53 stations—the subject of Hiroshige's most famous work. This series focuses on the people in those stations. The city of Hamamatsu (lit., "beach pine") is on the Pacific coast in Shizuoka Prefecture. In this print two women are seen against a background of pine trees on the beach; one carries a bamboo basket, the other a bamboo rake. Grunwald Center for the Graphic Arts, UCLA. Purchased from the Frank Lloyd Wright Collection. 1965.30.299O.

Plates 2, 3. Paintings from an illustrated scroll of flower arrangement (*rikka*), captioned *Old record showing secret points of flower arrangement.* Pigment on paper. Scroll size, 17.6 x 401.0 cm. Muromachi period, c. 1529. Artist: Sōsei. On this scroll, possibly the oldest document of *rikka*, 17 pictures depict appropriate arrangements for diverse occasions or places, each with brief commentary by the artist. The containers in Plate 2 are both in the "hanging boat" shape (*tsuribune*), a popular one for baskets. Courtesy of The Museum Yamato Bunkakan, Nara, Japan.

Plate 4. *The Chrysanthemum Festival - the Ninth Day of the Ninth Month.* Woodblock printed in red, tan, green, lilac, and pale blue, c. 1777. 26.2 x 39.2 cm. Artist: Isoda Koryūsai. Traditionally there are five festivals celebrating the times of year, each associated with its own plant(s): the 7th day of the first month with 7 grasses; the 3rd day of the 3rd month with peach blossom; the 5th day of the 5th month with iris; the 7th day of the 7th month with bamboo, and the 9th day of the 9th month, or Chōyō, with chrysanthemum. The first four are still part of Japanese life but Chōyō is rarely observed today. In this print, a courtesan and her attendant arrange flowers in a basket vase. Another painting on the theme of Chōyō by Katsukawa Shunshō (1726-1792) likewise shows chrysanthemums in a basket. Baskets rather than vases seem to have been favored for the display of chrysanthemums. Clarence Buckingham Collection 1924.2227. © Art Institute of Chicago. All Rights Reserved.

Plate 5. *Looking at a hanging scroll by Okumura Masanobu.* Color print. Chuban. Artist: Suzuki Harunobu (17??-1770). Plums and camellias, arranged in a hanging basket on the *tokonoma* column (*tokobashira*) give a feeling of early spring to this print. A woman, probably a courtesan, examines a scroll and may be contemplating the next painting to adorn the *tokonoma*. Harunobu was an influential Ukiyoe ("Floating World") artist who poetically depicted the lives of people in the Edo period. Kabuki actors and beautiful women, especially courtesans, were common themes of the Ukiyoe artists. Harunobu was the originator, in 1765, of the multi-colored woodcut. Spaulding Collection. Museum of Fine Arts, Boston. 21.4505.

Plate 6. A contemporary *tokonoma* with tea flowers in a basket (Pl. 9) photographed at the house of Los Angeles tea master Sōsei Matsumoto. Scroll by Hōunsai, Kyoto grand master of the Urasenke tea ceremony. May 1988.

Plate 7. Double-walled pail-shaped bamboo container (*hanaire*). Bamboo, rattan. 55.8 cm.

Technically in the category of *marutake kumi-mono*, this container is mat plaited on the inside, but its outside is constructed of bamboo tubes left whole at either end and halved elsewhere so as to be flush against the surface. Lent by Helen and Robert Kuhn.

Plate 8a. Flower basket (*hanakago*) in the *karamono* style. Bamboo, rattan. 53.0 cm. Signature: Chikukōen.
The handle, symmetry and intricacy are typical of *karamono*. In particular, the open constructions at the shoulder and continuous circular forms at the high base give it a Chinese flavor. The signature "Chikukōen" is not that of an individual basket maker, but that of a studio owned by relatives of Hayakawa Shōkosai.
UCLA MCH X87-176.
Gift of Nancy and Richard Bloch.

Plate 8b. Flower basket (*hanakago*) in the *karamono* style. Bamboo, rattan. 49.5 cm. Signature: Shōbun.
In its distinctive handles and globular body, the shape of this piece replicates a much-copied original from China, which has been owned for centuries by a temple in Kyoto, and is named Reishōjo after the legendary woman taken by basket makers as their founding deity. While the original has open work only on one part of its body, this piece has it over all, showing the maker's individuality. A Reishōjo basket looks particularly good with peonies (*botan*), and is thus also called *botankago* ("peony basket"). The rim exemplifies *atebuchi* wrapping. Lent by the Neutrogena Corporation.

Plate 9. Flower basket (*hanaire*) of the type called Sōzen Kago, after the original maker of the type. Bamboo. 30.0 cm. Signature illegible.
The Sōzen Kago is generally used for flowers in *chanoyu*. Roughly crafted compared to the minute, elaborate style of *karamono*), it exemplifies the Japanese-style *wagumi* basket used for tea ceremony flowers (see Pl. 6). UCLA MCH X87-188. Gift of Nancy and Richard Bloch.

Plate 10. *Flowers and fruit in a basket (Ranchū kakazu).* Water color on silk. 84.4 x 36.5 cm. Artist: Yanagisawa Kien (1704-1758). A literati painter, Kien often chose the theme of decorative flowers for his paintings. This kind of arrangement, with flowers and fruit in a *morikago*, must have given artistic focus to the *tokonoma* for the *sencha* ceremony among the cultured class. Anonymous collection, Japan. Published in *Bunjinga suihen*, vol. 11. *Gion Nankai. Yanagisawa Kien.* Tokyo, 1976. Courtesy of Chūōkōron-sha, publisher.

Plate 11a. Fruit basket (*morikago*) with handle. Bamboo and rattan. 44.5 cm. *Morikago* are sometimes used for fruit display during the *senchadō* ceremony. This basket has a raft bottom (*ikadazoko*, see Fig. 22) and butterfly knots (*chō-musubi*) appear on the handle. Flowers, too, can be displayed in this kind of basket. Lent by Helen and Robert Kuhn.

Plate 11b. Fruit basket (*morikago*) with handle. Bamboo. 30.0 cm. Signature: Shōkosai. Lent by Helen and Robert Kuhn.

Plate 12. Flower basket (*hanakago*) with handle. Bamboo, rattan. 51.0 cm. Signature: Shōkosai.
This may be a piece by Hayakawa Shōkosai I, who developed a Japanese flavor in basketry at a time when *hanakago* were often copies of Chinese imports. His use of bamboo tube at the corners seems original when combined with the delicate interlacing, decorative knots, and wrapping.
UCLA MCH X87-214.
Gift of Nancy and Richard Bloch.

Plate 13. Flower basket (*hanakago*). Bamboo, rattan. 40.6 cm. Signature: Chikuhōsai.
For the basket frame a wide, thick strip of bamboo and two pieces of rattan, cut in half, are bent into a circular form. Between these frames there is minute, elegant lozenge plaiting, mat plaiting, and twining. The body is further decorated with fancy wrapping and knots. The three works by Maeda Chikuhōsai I exhibited here (see also Pl. 14) each demonstrate a different style. Lent by the Neutrogena Corporation.

Plate 14a. Flower basket (*hanakago*) with handle. Sooted bamboo (*susutake*), bamboo rhizome, rattan. 49.0 cm. Signature: Chikuhōsai.
This basket illustrates a double hexagonal plaiting technique, with two strips for each mesh instead of one. Although the plaiting of the wide strips is relaxed, the elaborate rattan wraps and knots are well integrated into the whole body. Chikuhōsai also produced extremely minute, refined work (see Pl. 13). UCLA MCH X87-195. Gift of Nancy and Richard Bloch.

Plate 14b. Double-walled pail-shaped flower container (*hanaire*). Bamboo, rattan. 50.5 cm. Signature: Chikuhōsai.
The inside wall is worked in hexagonal plaiting; the outside is made with strips of varying widths, vertically inserted, and horizontal strips plaited along the vertical strips to secure them. Lent by Helen and Robert Kuhn.

Plate 15a. Flower basket (*hanakago*) with handle. Bamboo, tree root, rattan. 48.0 cm. The bottom is crysanthemum-plaited (*kiku-ami*, see Fig. 20) and the base is mat-plaited. Wide strips are vertically inserted (*tatezashi*) over the base structure. At the middle of the body, more narrow strips, inserted diagonally, hold the vertical ones and create a pleasing design. Lent by Helen and Robert Kuhn.

Plate 15b. Flower basket (*hanakago*) with handle. Bamboo, tree root, rattan. 58.0 cm. This is another example of *tatezashi*. Lent by Helen and Robert Kuhn.

Plate 16. Flower basket (*hanakago*). Bamboo. 38.0 cm. This basket exemplifies an insertion technique in the herringbone or "arrowtail" pattern (*yahazuzashi*), each piece of which is a separate element inserted into the body. Lent by Helen and Robert Kuhn.

Plate 17. Flower basket (*hanakago*) with handle. Leached bamboo (*sarashidake*) and rattan. 48.5 cm. Signature: Chikuyūsai. The entire body is done in a 2/2 twill plaiting technique (see detail, Fig. 26) with six thick bamboo strips attached. The rim exemplifies *makibuchi*. The yellowish white color of the leached bamboo emphasizes its simple beauty. Lent by Helen and Robert Kuhn.

Plate 18. Flower basket (*hanakago*). Sooted bamboo (*susutake*), rattan. 31.8 cm. Signature: Kōchikusai. Like the *wagumi* baskets used in *chanoyu*, this basket is plaited in a relaxed lozenge pattern with rather wide strips, in contrast to the elaborate and minute constructions of *karamono* style. Lent by the Neutrogena Corporation.

90

Plate 19. Flower basket (*hanakago*) with handle. Bamboo, rattan. 45.5 cm. The bottom is done in square plaiting (*yotsume-ami*, see detail, Fig. 18). Lent by Helen and Robert Kuhn.

Plate 20. Flower basket (*hanakago*) with hexagonal shoulder projection. Bamboo, rattan. 30.5 cm. Signature: Shokushōsai. The body is done in hexagonal plaiting (*mutsume-ami*, see detail, Fig. 19). Lent by the Neutrogena Corporation.

Plate 21. Flower basket (*hanakago*) with handle. Bamboo, rattan. 55.9 cm. Signature: Shokushōsai. Though the basketwork—a combination of lozenge plaiting and twining (*nawa-ami*)—appears plain, strips are extremely thin and narrow, and thus difficult to work with. Both simple wrapping (*bō-maki*, see detail, Fig. 32) and interlocking 'V' knots (*kunoji-musubi*, see detail, Fig. 38) appear on the handle. Suzuki Shokushōsai was an active basket maker in Tokyo during the first three decades of the twentieth century. Lent by the Neutrogena Corporation.

Plate 22. Flower basket (*hanakago*) with handle. Bamboo, rattan. 45.7 cm. Signature: Hōsai. Except under the rim, this basket is entirely twill plaited (*ajiro-ami*, see detail, Fig. 21). The rice-character stitch (*kome-no-ji-dome*, see detail, Fig. 42) can be seen on the ribs of the body. Lent by the Neutrogena Corporation.

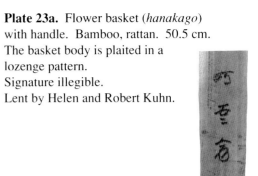

Plate 23a. Flower basket (*hanakago*) with handle. Bamboo, rattan. 50.5 cm. The basket body is plaited in a lozenge pattern. Signature illegible. Lent by Helen and Robert Kuhn.

Plate 23b. Flower basket (*hanakago*) with handle. Bamboo, rattan. 52.5 cm. This piece displays wrapped hexagonal plaiting (see detail, Fig. 24). Lent by Helen and Robert Kuhn.

Plate 23c. Flower basket (*hanakago*) with handle. Bamboo, rattan. 55.9 cm. In this basket various intervals of strip pass-overs create interesting twill-plaited patterns. The rim demonstrates *atebuchi* wrapping (see detail, Fig. 30). Insect wrapping (*mushi-maki*, see detail, Fig. 34), spiral cross knot (*jūji-uzumaki-musubi*, see detail, Fig. 37), and double interlocking 'V' knot (see detail, Fig. 39) appear on the handle. Lent by the Neutrogena Corporation.

Plate 24a. Flower basket (*hanakago*) with gourd decorations. Bamboo, rattan. 58.7 cm. The entire body is very finely mat plaited (*gozame-ami*, see detail, Fig. 27), with careful attention to the delicate and complex treatment of wraps and knots, especially around the rim, handle, and foot attachment. Lent by the Neutrogena Corporation.

Plate 24b. Flower basket (*hanakago*) with handle. Bamboo. 50.0 cm. Note the twining (*nawa-ami*, see detail, Fig. 28) on the lower part of the body. UCLA MCH X87-216. Gift of Nancy and Richard Bloch.

Plate 25. Flower basket (*hanakago*) with handle. Leached bamboo. 47.5 cm. Irregular plaiting (*midare*) produces a powerful, expressionistic character, and the use of several layers of strips intensifies the feeling of strength and solidity. Lent by Helen and Robert Kuhn.

Plate 26a. Flower basket (*hanakago*) with projected flat rim. Bamboo, rattan. 38.0 cm. A variety of insertion techniques can be observed: wide strips are inserted vertically at the body (*tatezashi*), and diagonal ones at the shoulder. Lent by Robert and Helen Kuhn.

Plate 26b. Turnip-shaped flower basket (*hanakago*). Bamboo. 26.5 cm. Lent by Helen and Robert Kuhn.

Plate 27. Flower basket (*hanakago*) with handle. Bamboo and tree root. 38.5 cm. Strips of different widths and different shades of rich brown are inserted diagonally into the hexagonal body structure to produce a powerful appeal. Body strips are extended and manipulated to form the rim, exemplifying *tomobuchi*. The rough, crooked form of the tree-root handle is a distinctive accent matching the lively mood of the body. Lent by Helen and Robert Kuhn.

Plate 28. Double-walled fruit basket (*morikago*) with handle. Bamboo. 32.0 cm. Lent by Helen and Robert Kuhn.

Plate 29. Double-walled flower basket (*hanakago*) with flat projecting rim. Bamboo, rattan. 45.7 cm. This basket shows various insertion techniques; the plain twill plaiting of the inner wall supports the outer one. Lent by the Neutrogena Corporation.

Plate 30a. Gourd-shaped flower basket (*hanakago*). Bamboo, rattan. 31.5 cm. The rim demonstrates *atebuchi* wrapping. Lent by Helen and Robert Kuhn.

Plate 30b. Flower basket (*hanakago*) in *karamono* style. Bamboo, rattan. 61.0 cm. Signature illegible. The rim shows *atebuchi* wrapping. Stitched insect wrapping (*kakemushi-maki*) appears on the handle (see detail, Fig. 35). Lent by the Neutrogena Corporation.

Plate 30c. Flower basket (*hanakago*) with handle. Bamboo, rattan, vine. 55.0 cm. The four bamboo pieces attached to the body of this basket may be sooted bamboo (*susutake*), which is often smoked for more than a century as part of the frame of a traditional thatched house. The parts with lighter shade were probably covered by the cordage that bound the bamboo frames. Lent by Helen and Robert Kuhn.

Plate 31a. Flower basket (*hanakago*) with handle. Bamboo. 30.5 cm. Lent by the Neutrogena Corporation.

Plate 31b. Flower basket (*hanakago*). Bamboo, rattan. 33.0 cm. A great number of narrow strips are plaited in an irregular way, producing a bird's nest effect. Lent by the Neutrogena Corporation.

Plate 32. Flower basket (*hanakago*) with handle. Bamboo, rattan. 86.4 cm. This very decorative basket has many kinds of elaborate knots and wrappings (for example, *sujiiri bō-maki*, wrapping with design, and *kame-no-ko-musubi*, turtle-shell knot, see Figs. 33, 41) applied to its body as well as its exceptionally large handle. Lent by the Neutrogena Corporation.

Plate 33a. Double-walled flower basket (*hanakago*) with handle. Bamboo, tree root, rattan. 68.6 cm. Lent by the Neutrogena Corporation.

Plate 33b. Double-walled flower basket (*hanakago*). Bamboo, rattan. 40.0 cm. Lent by the Neutrogena Corporation.

Plate 33c. Double-walled flower basket (*hanakago*). Bamboo, rattan. 39.0 cm. Narrow strips are bunched together and inserted to produce a wave-like pattern on its globular body. Since the ocean-wave pattern (*seigaiha*) is an auspicious symbol in Japanese art iconography, this basket may have been used for a special occasion. The outer wall with its extensive insertions is supported by an inner wall. Lent by Helen and Robert Kuhn.

Plate 34a. Flower basket (*hanakago*). Bamboo. 42.5 cm. Lent by Helen and Robert Kuhn.

Plate 34b. Flower basket (*hanakago*) with handle. Bamboo. 47.0 cm. The inside is done in hexagonal plaiting and twining; bamboo strips are inserted diagonally into the open spaces. Lent by the Neutrogena Corporation.

Plate 35a. Flower basket (*hanakago*) with handle. Bamboo. 42.0 cm. Lent by Helen and Robert Kuhn.

Plate 35b. Flower basket (*hanakago*) with projecting rim. Bamboo. 25.5 cm. Lent by Helen and Robert Kuhn.

91

Plate 35c. Flower basket (*hanakago*) with handle. Bamboo. 43.2 cm. Signature: Kenryōsai. Lent by the Neutrogena Corporation.

Plate 36a. Flower basket (*hanakago*) with handle. Bamboo. 56.5 cm. The handle is made from twisted bamboo cordage. Lent by Helen and Robert Kuhn.

Plate 36b. Flower basket (*hanakago*) with handle. Bamboo, rattan. 48.0 cm. Signature: Shinsai. Very thin strips are delicately manipulated to produce a gently curved, perfect body in openwork. Lent by Helen and Robert Kuhn.

Plate 36c. Flower basket (*hanakago*) with handle. Bamboo, rattan. 52.1 cm. Signature: Chikuichisai. Lent by the Neutrogena Corporation.

92

Plate 37a. Flower basket (*hanakago*) with handle. Bamboo. 52.0 cm. Lent by Helen and Robert Kuhn.

Plate 37b. Flower basket (*hanakago*). Bamboo and rattan. 31.0 cm. This piece borrows its shape from a celadon vase with ears, and herringbone inserting gives the body an appealing texture. Lent by Helen and Robert Kuhn.

Plate 38. Boat-shaped flower basket (*hanakago*). Bamboo, rattan. 52.0 cm. Signature illegible. Originally from China, the boat shape is a popular one for Japanese flower baskets. UCLA MCH X87-185. Gift of Nancy and Richard Bloch.

Plate 39a. Flower basket (*hanakago*). Bamboo, rattan. 52.0 cm. Signature: Kōgetsu. UCLA MCH X87-172. Gift of Nancy and Richard Bloch.

Plate 39b. Flower basket (*hanakago*) with handle. Bamboo, tree root, rattan. 77.5 cm. The inside is twill-plaited. Wide bamboo strips, attached at the base, are split at the upper part of the body into narrower pieces. These are further plaited in complicated forms, the ends of which are inserted into the base structures. The dynamic composition of the wide strips gives this piece a sculptural quality. Lent by the Neutrogena Corporation.

Plate 39c. Flower basket (*hanakago*). Bamboo, rattan. 82.0 cm. Signature: Tōshōsai. Double interlocking 'V' knots appear on the handle. UCLA MCH X87-227. Gift of Nancy and Richard Bloch.

Plate 40a. Flower basket (*hanakago*) with handle. Bamboo, tree root. 47.0 cm. Lent by the Neutrogena Corporation.

Plate 40b. Flower basket (*hanakago*) with handle. Bamboo, bamboo rhizome, rattan. 41.0 cm. Signature: Chikuhōsai. The rim and vertical strips of the body are wrapped with cordage. Lent by Helen and Robert Kuhn.

Plate 40c. Flower basket (*hanakago*). Bamboo. 39.5 cm. Cords made of extremely thin, narrow bamboo strips are worked into the four corners of the basket and folded into complicated forms at the base, where they serve as feet. Lent by Helen and Robert Kuhn.

Plate 41a. Flower basket (*hanakago*) with handle. Bamboo. 46.0 cm. Multiple layers of wefts produce a three-dimensional effect on the surface of the body. Lent by Helen and Robert Kuhn.

Plate 41b. Flower basket (*hanakago*) with handle. Bamboo. 48.5 cm. Lent by Helen and Robert Kuhn.

Plate 42a. Hanging flower basket (*hanakago*). Bamboo, vine. 34.3 cm. Lent by the Neutrogena Corporation.

Plate 42b. Hanging flower basket (*hanakago*). Bamboo, rattan. 16.5 cm. Signature: Hōnan.
This exemplifies the Japanese rustic style called *wagumi* and associated with *chanoyu*. Sides and bottom are square plaited; front and back of the body are twill plaited, but strip-movement intervals are not as regular as in the usual twill plaiting, which gives the piece a relaxed, spontaneous mood. Lent by Belinda Sweet.

Plate 42c. Hanging gourd-shaped flower basket (*hanakago*). Bamboo. 44.5 cm. Lent by the Neutrogena Corporation.

Plate 43a. Hanging double-walled flower basket (*hanakago*) in the moon shape. Bamboo, rattan. 34.3 cm. Lent by the Neutrogena Corporation.

Plate 43b. Hanging double-walled flower basket (*hanakago*). Bamboo, rattan. 41.0 cm. The extremely thin, narrow strips used in this basket make it exceptionally light. UCLA MCH X87-184. Gift of Nancy and Richard Bloch.

Plate 44a. Shell-shaped fruit basket (*morikago*). Bamboo, tree root. 38.6 cm. The twill plaiting at the base of this basket produces a six-pointed star pattern. Lent by the Neutrogena Corporation.

Plate 44b. Flower basket (*hanakago*) with handle. Bamboo. 33.0 cm. Signature: Hōchiku. Lent by the Neutrogena Corporation.

Plate 45a. Double-walled flower basket (*hanakago*) with handle. Bamboo, bamboo rhizome, rattan. 48.3 cm. Signature illegible. Lent by the Neutrogena Corporation.

Plate 45b. Flower basket (*hanakago*) with handle. Bamboo, bamboo rhizome, rattan. 40.6 cm. Signature: Chikuichisai. Lent by the Neutrogena Corporation.

Plate 45c. Flower basket (*hanakago*) with handle. Bamboo, rattan. 57.0 cm. Signature: Kōchikusai.
The insect stitch, *mushi-kagari* (see detail, Fig. 43) adorns the body ribs, which also serve as feet. Lent by Helen and Robert Kuhn.

Plate 46. Flower basket (*hanakago*). Bamboo, rattan. 34.9 cm. Lent by the Neutrogena Corporation.

Plate 47a. Flower basket (*hanakago*) with handle. Bamboo, vine. 46.5 cm. Lent by Helen and Robert Kuhn.

Plate 47b. Flower basket (*hanakago*) with handle. Bamboo, tree root, rattan. 47.0 cm. Lent by Helen and Robert Kuhn.

93

Glossary

ami, interworking of elements in non-woven textiles, hence plaiting, twining, laceworking, netting, matting, knitting, crocheting, etcetera

ajiro-ami, twill plaiting

asa-no-ha, hemp leaf pattern, an application of hexagonal plaiting

atebuchi, rim technique in which wide bamboo strips encircle rim to hold end of body strips

cha, tea

chabana, flower arrangement for *chanoyu*

chadō, lit., "the way of tea"; the tea ceremony with *matcha*; also, its associated way of life or philosophy

chanoyu, lit., "tea in hot water"; the tea ceremony developed in the Muromachi period using powdered tea (*matcha*)

furo, portable brazier used to boil water for *chanoyu*

gozame-ami, mat plaiting (one method of producing *mawashimono*)

gyō, of medium formality, between *shin* and *sō*; a concept with originally applied to calligraphy, gradually extended to architecture and art forms of all kinds in Japanese life

hachiku, *Pyllostachy nigra*, a species of bamboo sometimes used for baskets

hagi (or *hegi*), stripping (of bamboo)

hana, flower

hanaire, lit., "flower container," general term for all classes of flower container, also applied to a container in the tea ceremony context

hanakago, flower basket

haritake (or *chikaratake*), thick, wide bamboo pieces used for insertion to strengthen the bottom of a basket

henso, technical classification of baskets (and other technically non-woven objects such as mats) made by plaiting, twining, matting, etcetera

hirahagi, a process in which outer & inner surfaces of bamboo are stripped in preparation for basket making

ikebana, [the art of] flower arrangement

isshi sōden, the handing down of specialized knowledge and techniques from father to child (usually eldest son)

kago, basket

karamono, lit., "Chinese objects," general term describing decorative items—vases, utensils, baskets—imported from China

kōgei, lit., "craft art" (as distinguished from "pure art," e.g. painting)

kiku-ami, crysanthemum plaiting

kumi, [artistic] composition

makibuchi, rim technique wherein body strips are held in cores, then wrapped

madake, (*Phyllostachys bambusoides*), the commonest species of Japanese bamboo, most commonly used for baskets

masawari, stripping process in which bamboo is split laterally into very narrow pieces

marutakemono, lit., "a thing made of bamboo tube," a bamboo tube vase

marutake kumimono, lit., "a thing constructed of bamboo tubes," a basket made of bamboo tubes

matcha, powdered green tea

mawashimono, basket work in which warps are wider than wefts, or are double

medake, *Arundinaria simonii*, species of bamboo used for baskets

midare, irregular plaiting

morikago, shallow basket for display of fruit, and sometimes flowers

mutsume-ami, hexagonal or six-mesh plaiting

nawa-ami, twining (one method of producing *mawashimono*)

nemagaridake, *Sasa kurilensis*, species of bamboo used in basketry

rantai-shikki, heavily lacquered baskets

ro, winter fire pit used to boil water for *chanoyu*

sarashidake, leached bamboo

sencha, tea brewed from tea leaves

senchadō, lit., "the way of sencha"; the tea ceremony developed in the Edo period using *sencha* tea; also its associated way of life or philosophy

shin, formal (see *gyō*)

shoin, study or reception room—feature of Muromachi era mansions

sō, informal or relaxed in form (see *gyō*)

sōan, grass hut

sashi, inscrtion

susutake, sooted bamboo (of any species)

suzutake, *Bambusa brealis*, a species of bamboo commonly used for baskets

tabane-ami, bundle plaiting

take, bamboo (generic name)

takekōgei, lit., "bamboo craft art," (contemporary term) bamboo art

takekōgeika, lit.,"bamboo craft artist," bamboo artist

tatezashi, insertion pattern showing straight vertical lines

tenmoku, type of shallow, glazed *karamono* tea bowl used in *chanoyu*.

tokonoma, alcove, special area of house expressing family aesthetic, reserved for display of scroll, *ikebana*, incense, and other ornaments.

tomobuchi, rim technique in which body strips are extended, manipulated, and bent to form rim

tomokumimono, basket work composed of same width bamboo strips

wagumi, simple, rough Japanese-style basketry associated with *chanoyu*

wari, splitting (of bamboo)

yahazuzashi, lit., "arrowtail inserting"; an insertion technique creating the pattern that Westerners term herringbone

yotsume-ami, square or four-mesh plaiting

94

Bibliography

Adovasio, J. M.
1977 *Basketry Technology, A Guide to Identification and Analysis.* Chicago.

Castile, Rand
1971 *The Way of Tea.* New York.

Farrelly, David
1984 *The Book of Bamboo.* San Francisco.

Fujioka Ryōichi
1968 *Nihon no bijutsu, No. 22, Chadōgu* (Japanese art, No. 22, Tea ceremony utensils). Tokyo. In translation: *Tea Ceremony Utensils.* Louise Allison Cort (transl.). New York 1973.

Iijima Isamu
1966 *Nihon no bijutsu, No. 4, Bunjinga* (Japanese art, No. 4, Literati painting). Tokyo.

Ikeda Hyōa
1968 *Take no shugei* (Bamboo craft). Tokyo.
1980 *Chikugei henreki: chashaku, hanaire, kago* (Tour through bamboo crafts: tea scoops, flower containers, baskets). Kyoto.
1985 *Chadōgu no tanoshimi* (Joy of tea ceremony utensils). Tokyo.

Ikeda Hyōa & Ikeda Kiyoshi
1987 "Chaseki no kago: kagoamimono no yō to bi o megutte" (Tea cere- mony baskets: their function and beauty). In *Nagomi*, July 1987:5-47.

Ienaga Saburō (ed.)
1966 *Nihon bunkashi 4, Muromachi-jidai* (Cultural history of Japan 4, Muromachi period). Tokyo.

Keene, Donald (trans.)
1956 "The Tale of the Bamboo Cutter." *Monumenta Nipponica* 11(4):329-355.

Mizuo Hiroshi
1970 *Nihon no zōkei 2, takehen* (Japanese art form 2, bamboo). Kyoto.

Ogasawara Yoshihiko
1985 "Amimono. Nuno" (Plaitings. Texture). In *Jōmon bunka no kenkyu 7, dōgu to gijutsu*: 293-304 (Studies on Jōmon culture 7, tools and technology.) Katō Shinpei, Kobayashi Tatsuo and Fujimoto Tsuyoshi (eds.). Tokyo.

Ogawa Kōraku
1980 *Cha no bunkashi* (Cultural history of tea). Tokyo.
1986 *Sencha seki no hana* (Flowers in *sencha* tea ceremony). Osaka.

Ōi Minobu
1964 *Ikebana Graphic: seikatsu kara mita ikebana no rekishi* (Ikebana Graphic; history of *ikebana* from the perspective of Japanese life). Tokyo.

Osabe Michihiko, Shiraishi Kazumi, Kaneko Kenji and Moroyama Masanori
1985 *Take no kōgei—kindai ni okeru tenkai: "Modern Bamboo Craft."* Exhibition Catalogue, The National Museum of Modern Art. Tokyo.

Satō Shōgorō
1974 *Zusetsu takekōgei: take kara takekōgeihin made* (Illustrated guide to bamboo craft: from bamboo to bamboo crafts). Tokyo.

Sekijima Hisako
1986 *Basketry - Projects from Baskets to Grass Slippers.* Tokyo.

Ueda Kōichirō
1979 *Take to nihonjin* (Bamboo and the Japanese People). Tokyo.

Watanuki Kiyoshi
1985 "Take yōzai" (Bamboo materials) and "Takekōgeihin" (Bamboo crafts). In *Mokuchiku-kōgei no jiten*: 90-94, 484-98 (Dictionary of wooden and bamboo craft). Yanagi Munemichi, Shibuya Tadashi, Uchibori Shigeo (eds.). Tokyo.

Yagihashi Makoto, Shiraishi Kazumi, and Ōtaki Mikio
1986 *Nihon no waza: ningen kokuhō ni yoru tokubetsu-ten* (Works in Japan: special exhibition by the Living National Treasures). Exhibition catalogue, Sano Museum. Mishima, Japan.

Yamane Yūzō
1987 "Geinō to shiteno ikebana no seiritsu to tenkai" (The foundation and development of *ikebana* as art form). In *Nihon bijutsu-kōgei* (9) 588: 15-23 (Japanese craft art).

Credits

All studio photographs not otherwise credited were taken by Richard Todd. Field photographs of bamboo artists and their work were taken by Toshiko M. McCallum. Sketches, map, and chart were produced by Jung-yu S. Lien, who designed the entire volume on Macintosh II using Page-maker 2.0a. The book was output on a Linotronics L300 by Associated Students UCLA Typography Department. Alan Lithograph Inc. did the color separations and printing. The volume was bound by Roswell Bookbinding Company.